tho' I am very glad to be up here again free from all suggestion of any of my responsibilities. Nothing rests one like that. In spite of rainy weather the valley is supremely beautiful still, and I took more of a walk yesterday than I have perpetrated since 1899, with no distress or after symptoms of fatigue. It makes me feel quite happy, to "climb a bit once more. Alice has been extraordinarily well, both physically and morally, for three months past, and Peggy's quiet summer has doubtless done her good. We spent nearly a month in the beautiful town of Lincoln, in Harry Warner's breezily and

the thing was *not* to be
western journey was (the
complication of my having to go
to N.Y. remuneratedly to lecture
of the mere scrap of time left
by the them so doodish & the
foregoing Roberts) too brief &
rather for an extended impression,
an abiding saturation, a
accumulation of Notes & there
in this wouldn't have permitted
doing something Could I have
at that part of my scheme
tely. the earlier ~~part~~ may of the sa
me till so much time h
that here, & at a distance
out of actual touch the
whole thing had fa

Wᵐ & H'ry

MUSE
BOOKS
THE IOWA SERIES
IN CREATIVITY &
· WRITING

ROBERT D.
RICHARDSON
series editor

W<u>m</u> *&* H'ry

Literature, Love, and the Letters between
WILLIAM *&* HENRY JAMES

by
J. C. HALLMAN

UNIVERSITY OF IOWA PRESS
IOWA CITY

S

191
JAM

University of Iowa Press, Iowa City 52242
Copyright © 2013 by J. C. Hallman
www.uiowapress.org
Printed in the United States of America
Design by Sara T. Sauers

The University of Iowa Press is a member of Green Press Initiative
and is committed to preserving natural resources.
Printed on acid-free paper

Library of Congress Cataloging-in-Publication Data
Hallman, J. C.
Wm & H'ry: literature, love, and the letters between William and
Henry James / by J. C. Hallman.
     p.   cm.—(Muse books: the Iowa series in creativity and writing)
Includes bibliographical references and index.
ISBN-13: 978-1-60938-151-6 (cloth)
ISBN-10: 1-60938-151-3 (cloth)
ISBN-13: 978-1-60938-152-3 (e-book)
ISBN-10: 1-60938-152-1 (e-book)
1. James, William, 1842–1910—Family. 2. James, William, 1842–1910—
Correspondence. 3. Philosophers—United States—Correspondence.
4. Psychologists—United States—Correspondence. 5. James, Henry,
1843–1916—Family. 6. James, Henry, 1843–1916—Correspondence.
7. Authors, American—19th century—Correspondence. 8. Brothers—
United States—Correspondence. I. Title. II. Title: William and Henry.
B945.J24H22 2013
191—dc23   2012031166

It would seem just to say, then, that the bequests of Henry and William James have become so intricately woven into the pattern of contemporary literature that only an eagle and argus-eyed critic can hope to tease them out.—C. Hartley Grattan, *The Three Jameses*

TO WHOM IT MAY CONCERN,

For a short time a few years ago, funded almost exclusively by a modest advance for a book about W$^{\underline{m}}$ James, I lived a meager life in West Philadelphia. I rather enjoyed this. My dog and I walked daily to the outdoor tables of a Vietnamese restaurant for cheap lunches, and I happily sacrificed the comforts of a steady income to dedicate myself to work. There is a degree of irony to a man enduring poverty so he can study the thought of another whose life was mostly affluent—one who has even been accused of stinginess, though I don't agree with the charge—but I didn't think much about it then, and don't wish to make hay of it now. For whatever reason, the same trying days one strives to avoid tend to be, in retrospect, the happiest of days. I was happy then.

Part of this happiness, surely, owes to the fact that I had managed to convince the Free Library of Philadelphia to lend out its noncirculating copies of the then–newly published correspondence of W$^{\underline{m}}$ James. Even though many of the James family letters had been burned to preserve family

secrets (the original plan called for the unburned correspondence to be withheld from the public eye until the year
2022), W^m's collected letters came in at a shelf-bending
twelve volumes. During my time in Philadelphia eleven
of these volumes had been published; the first three were
dedicated to W^m and H'ry's lifelong exchange. I knew
at once that these particular books were remarkable—I
believe there exists no other epistolary commingling of
minds as complete between figures that have each proven
so influential—but I actually skipped them the first time
around. I started reading with Volume Four, the earli-
est of W^m's letters. For the better part of a year, I carried
those cinder-block books around in my satchel, their stiff
library binding gouging my lower back as I biked around
town. I humped them everywhere, like a penance. At first,
I read them at odd moments: before sleep, at bars, waiting
for subways, etc. Before long, however, the letters began
to feel intended for me, addressed to me, and soon I read
them not just at odd moments, but at completely normal
moments as well. I paced myself—I did not want to gobble
them—but of course I read them much more quickly than
had their original recipients. This has its advantages, and
it may be that the bare intimacy and raw wisdom of letters
stand out in greater relief at fast-forward.

A few years before W^m and H'ry were born, Ralph Waldo Emerson weighed these very things—letters, bareness and rawness, intimacy and wisdom—in a rare meditation on his own writing. Emerson criticized his essays; he feared that they had been pulled along with a culture-wide lurch toward staid, scholarly prose. Better was his correspondence, he thought. He was most fond of letters addressed "to anyone whom I love."

Emerson's longing for intimate letters offers a clear contrast to modern "correspondence," such that it is. The infection of monotone prose appears to have grown only more virulent, more gangrenous, and whatever we write these days, be it letters, or memos, or blogs, either electronic or "hard," is not addressed to those whom we love—rather, it is "released" to whomever it may concern.

I think that's why I began to feel as though W^m's letters were addressed to me: because no other letters were addressed to me.

As I neared the end of writing my book, a crisis loomed. Volume Twelve had just been released, but the library had not yet processed its copy. The librarians couldn't give it to me. I absolutely needed to read the last of W^m's letters, but Volume Twelve alone would cost $150. I was poor, if you'll recall, but I considered making the purchase. A little *tinkering revealed an even more tantalizing investment opportunity: the* entire set *could be got for $315, which was then about half my net worth. I debated for a while, and put in the order. I anxiously awaited the books' arrival. I paced at home each day, tried to anticipate the mailman's routine. This was ridiculous, since I'd already read most of the letters, and I was, in a sense, awaiting their arrival a second time. When the box finally came, I experienced the thrill of anticipated packages—a joy that is the timelessness of wonder, a tracing back to the source of imagination.*

I tore through Volume Twelve, but oddly only ever dabbled in the three books of W^m and H'ry's letters. I finished my project, and since then the correspondence has been prominently displayed in whatever I've had that passes for a living room.

W^m & H'ry assumes at least a little preexisting knowledge. Generally, readers know the work of one brother much better than they know the work of the other, and often—even for quite savvy readers—the fact that they were brothers at all is the new part of the equation. The following may suffice as introduction for each:

*Henry James is the most pivotal author of the last
150 years. Working freelance with a monk's dedica-
tion, he produced a virtually endless set of stories,
novels, and criticism. A great deal of what we now
think of as artful fiction traces back to his most
ambitious work.*

*William James is the father of modern psychology,
the founder of pragmatism, and the author of a
seminal book on comparative religion. An artist
turned scientist and philosopher, he taught at Harvard for forty years. His work echoes across a vast
range of disciplines.*

In biographies, W$^{\underline{m}}$ *and H'ry's relationship tends to
be treated for only its oxymoronic extremes: it is a loving
rivalry. The letters are not newly published or explored,
but exclusive focus on the brothers' differences overlooks
common wombs both literal and intellectual, and forgets
a lifetime of mutual influence. To date, the letters have not
been mined for what the James family pyromaniac correspondence editors certainly felt to be the case: given the
brothers' influence on philosophy, religion, science, art,
and literature, the letters are a raw and intimate presaging*

of much of thinking of the twentieth century. Just as in my living room, the three cinder-block volumes of W^m and H'ry's letters have been admired and exalted, but not yet fully read for the story and the message that was the intent of their preservation.

W^m & H'ry

ON SEPTEMBER 7, 1861, having lately abandoned a dream of life as an artist and enrolled in Harvard's Lawrence Scientific School, W^m set out from his new, strange, rented room in Cambridge and walked mechanically to the P.O., hoping against all hope to find a letter from his brother. His box was empty. W^m turned heavily away. Before he could leave, he felt a modest touch. It was his landlord's young son, offering an envelope inscribed with familiar characters.

"Mr. James! This was in our box!"

W^m tore open H'ry's letter, read it right there in the post office. That evening, homesick and alone on a Saturday night, he began a reply: "Sweet was your letter & grateful to my eyes." The first letter of the surviving correspondence contains snippets in French, Latin, and Portuguese, alludes to Shakespeare, reports on a visit to a collection of sculptural casts at the Boston Atheneum, and attests to an absence of "equanimity" (the presence of which, many years later, W^m would count among the defining traits of mysticism). He was nineteen years old.

They wrote often. They wrote letters about reading letters, letters about how much time had passed since they had received a letter, letters that depicted the moment of their composition. W^m's first letter describes the table on which he writes (round, with a red and black cloth), specifies the number of windows in his room (five), inventories his bookcase ("my little array of printed wisdom covering nearly *one* of the shelves"), and lists "Drear and Chill Abode" as its return address.

The early letters often express frustration with the inability of words to truly convey experience. Correspondence pales beside conversation. Over the next few years, as W^m and H'ry each completed an initial solo Grand Tour, they cried out for each other's company.

H'ry, from Lucerne: "I'd give my right hand for an hour's talk with you."

H'ry, from Venice, six weeks later: "Among the letters which I found here on my arrival was a most valuable one from you . . . which made me ache to my spirit's core for half an hour's talk with you."

W^m, from Berlin: "What would n't I give to have a good long talk with you all at home."

W^m, from Dresden, after visiting the Gallery: "I'd

give a good deal to import you and hear how some of the things strike you."

In 1869, W^m advised H'ry, then in Geneva, not to yield to homesickness. "I wish I heard from you oftener," H'ry had written. W^m told him to pay no mind to ennui, noting that his own "heaviest days were full of instruction." The same letter opened with a borrowed stanza:

> O call my brother back to me,
> I cannot play alone
> The summer comes with flower & bee
> Where is my brother gone?

A few years later, W^m described H'ry as "my in many respects twin bro," which serves as a fair description of the image he once sketched in the margin of a letter illustrating the proposed sleeping arrangements for H'ry's then-impending visit to Cambridge:

The pleas for companionship persisted as W$^{\underline{m}}$ and H'ry grew older, taking up permanent residence on opposite sides of the Atlantic Ocean, and establishing very different social lives and almost completely incompatible aesthetics.

> 1876: "Your letter . . . quickened my frequent desire to converse with you."
>
> 1883: "I would give any thing to see you."
>
> 1886: "Would to God I could get over to see you . . . for about 24 hours."
>
> 1889: "I long to talk with you—of, as you say, a 100 things."
>
> 1896: "How I wish I could sit in your midst!"
>
> 1899: "Within the last couple of days I have wished you were nearer to me, that I might consult with you."

In 1893, both brothers having recently passed fifty years of age, W$^{\underline{m}}$ reflected on the James family's thinning ranks (mother, father, and two younger siblings having died in recent years), claiming that he now felt, more than ever before, that he and H'ry "formed part of a unity." He was moved to quote from Matthew Arnold's "The Future," which had been formative in other ways. ("Where the river in gleaming rings / sluggishly winds through the plain / . . . So is the mind of man" anticipates the "stream of consciousness" that W^m articulated and H'ry employed.) Moved at impending mortality, W^m lifted snippets from the poem's conclusion.

And the width of the waters, the hush . . .
. . . may strike peace to the soul of man on its breast,
As the pale waste widens around him,
As the stars come out and the night-wind
Brings up the stream
Murmurs and scents of the infinite sea.

They were closer to death, but not close. The exchange continued for another seventeen years. The letters contain spats, disagreements, and plenty of evidence of diverging intellects, but chart, too, a love growing ever fonder. In 1910, several months before W^m died, H'ry fell into a sour mood. He had been dabbling with a nutritional chewing cure fad that his brother had recommended, but now the cure had backfired, and he had been left with a stomach that had forgotten how to digest food. His letters took on a frantic tone; he streamed fear and loneliness. "Oh for a letter!" he cried. W^m made plans to visit. "An immense change for the better will come, I feel, with your advent," H'ry rejoiced. *"That* will be my cure."

W^m arrived to comfort his brother in May. He was dead by August. H'ry lived another six years.

·2·

They wrote frequently, with zeal, of illness, of intestines, of parasites, of orthopedic mystery. In 1867, when W^m made passage to France on the *Great Eastern*, H'ry couldn't wait for the first letter to arrive from Paris before writing himself. He was uninterested in impressions of the city. "I am more anxious than I can say to hear how you endured your journey . . . your back, *that* is what I want to hear about."

The trip interrupted W^m's medical training, which had begun in 1864. He graduated five years later, after tagging along on a South American expedition with Louis Agassiz and then spending a mostly idle year and a half in Europe. His medical training was incomplete—in later years, he distrusted doctors himself, and sampled a variety of unusual cures—but he happily dispensed advice to H'ry. Only fifteen months separated the brothers, but W^m's letters often strike a parental tone.

Once, in 1886, after H'ry had established himself in England and begun his dizzying churn of novels and criticism, W^m offered to send along a weight-lifting machine.

"[It] would be very welcome to me here," H'ry replied, "as I don't get exercise enough."

W^m sent the apparatus and a set of heavily annotated directions. A long accompanying letter explained how the device should be installed and employed. "There is *no* muscular combination which cannot be exercised on those weights," W^m opined, "and a quarter of an hour . . . of from 10 to 20 different movements will *wake one up* all through one's cubic contents." As to the care of the machine, W^m drew a small oil can in the margin—in case H'ry didn't know what an oil can looked like.

The "lifting cure" cut both ways, however. It served just as well as a metaphor for the toil of literary study. In 1901, W^m complained that work on *The Varieties of Religious Experience* had left him "tired as a man might tire of holding out a weight forever." Long before, H'ry had drawn a similar parallel in a long letter detailing a three-stage process he had devised to cure his ailing back:

1. A stage in which exercise must go on increasing until it entirely predominates & attains its maximum—even to not sleeping, if necessary.
2. A stage in which sitting, reading, writing &c. may be gradually introduced & allowed to share its empire.
3. A stage in which they will hold their own against it & subsist on an equal & finally a superior footing.

In other words, the real problem was the mysterious toll taken by language. Words and the body were incompatible, and the body had to be tricked into permitting prolonged literary work. H'ry once wrote of the "damnable nausea (as I call it for want of a better word) that continuous reading & writing bring on." A doctor advised him to diet, exercise, and "not read." In 1883, W^m noted that an absence of "head work" left him "consequently in excellent physical condition," and H'ry lauded mountain climbing because "you sweat the rhapsodical faculty out of you." Letters themselves, though often a kind of cure ("my spirits were revived by the arrival of a most blessedly brotherly letter"), were made from language and could therefore become their own illness. Both brothers complained of time lost to correspondence (W^m: "Have just written 15 letters"; H'ry: "[This] is the 11th letter . . . I have written this morning"), but for H'ry in particular they became a symptom, "the very blight and leak, as it were, of my existence." W^m always praised H'ry's letters, but reminded him often that he needn't feel obliged to write because there was plenty of him to take in through his regularly appearing stories and essays.

It wasn't always dire. W^m took a particular glee in revealing the most intimate details of whatever he suffered. Ringworms acquired en route to Rio de Janeiro "waved" across his face and neck with "undiminished fire." A six-week growing itch on his "pubes, etc." (the most subtle "etc." in letters) proved on inspection to be "a plague of *Lice*!!" "Painful boils on [his] loins" were a terrible bother—"Christian doctrine is nothing to them"—but the endless attention they inspired, observing and reobserving, poking and pressing, could "fill a day with quivering interest." (In 1890, H'ry congratulated W^m on the end of twelve years' work on *The Principles of Psychology:* "It must seem as good as the breaking of a boil.") Special, and playful, attention was reserved for all manner of digestive failure.

The malfunction could fall on the side of too much, as when W^m described a disagreeable mountaintop lunch followed by a three-hour descent "in state of active nausea & diarrhea," or too little, as when W^m recommended galvanic treatments with an intimate, possibly firsthand, description of an electrified pole "put inside the rectum."

W^m's work as a psychologist, philosopher, and religious scholar can be broadly understood as an attempt to document, and cure, the human condition. He employed H'ry as proto-patient throughout their lives, and was possibly even more interested in his brother's condition than the reverse. "I blush to say," he wrote (at age twenty-seven!), "that detailed bulletins of your bowels, stomach &c . . . are of the most enthralling interest to me." H'ry obliged, happily. In reply to the admonition *Never resist a motion to stool*, H'ry admitted, "I may actually say I *can't get a passage*. My 'little squirt' has ceased to have more than a nominal use." H'ry used the exchange for more than advice as to which parts of his body to submit to electroshock. Writing about illness became the laboratory in which he tested writerly theories. His later plots often hinge on whether characters are truly sick, and ailments, either mental or physical, were precisely the kind of citadel that language found it a challenge to breach ($W^{\underline{m}}$: "Sighs are hard to express in words"). H'ry's bowels were a perfect training ground for practicing elegant prose that described inelegant events.

A prolonged "crisis" of 1869 improved H'ry's pen if not his gut. He had suffered terribly through the first few months of his European tour. "Anti-bilious" pills had produced a "violent inclination to stool," but he only bled a little when he tried. A doctor assured him there was no obstruction ("by the insertion of his finger (horrid tale!)"), and he was left finally, in Florence, with the awareness that while he absolutely needed a movement he had no idea how to get one. More important than the cures he tried, however, was his meditation on the incident as a whole. His pages-long telling culminates in a climax of characteristic early-Jamesian prose:

These reflections fill me with a perfectly *passionate* desire for a reformation in my bowels. I see in it not only the question of a special localized affection, but a large general change in my condition & a blissful renovation of my life—the reappearance above the horizon of pleasures which had well-nigh sunk forever behind that great murky pile of undiminishing contingencies to which my gaze has so long been accustomed. It would result in the course of a comparatively short time, a return to repose—reading—hopes & ideas—an escape from this weary world of idleness.

W^m was not oblivious to the sly pun, and offered his own in return. He called the story a "moving intestinal drama," a characterization H'ry judged happily termed.

Even after the comic annoyance of youthful constipation, the correspondence maps the trajectory of the brothers' work. They each settled into philosophies and aesthetics, and each made consciousness a feature of their investigations. W^m wanted to pinpoint consciousness or at least find a way to describe it. H'ry sought to depict it, even in his letters. His epistolary output exploded with illness—he wrote *more* when he was sick. In 1910, the frenzied letters describing his latest digestive episode (a problem with his "physical consciousness"), the same letters that brought W^m

charging across the Atlantic to his doom, now depicted H'ry's raging interiority, the "constituted consciousness" that he had only recently described as the true novelist's "immense adventure":

But my diagnosis is, to myself, crystal clear— & would be in the last degree demonstrable if I could linger more. What happened was that I found myself at a given moment more & more beginning to fail of power to eat through the daily more marked increase of a strange & most persistent & depressing stomachic crisis: the condition of more & more sickishly *loathing* food. This weakened & undermined & "lowered" me, naturally, more & more—& finally scared me through rapid & extreme loss of flesh & increase of weakness & emptiness— failure of nourishment. I struggled in the wilderness, with occasional & delusive flickers of improvement . . . & then 18 days ago I collapsed and went to bed.

On October 13, 1876, H'ry scribbled out a quick reply
to W^m's previous two letters. The first of these had
described a battle with dysentery that W^m had waged
after a country rest, and the second made a peculiar
request: could H'ry please obtain a perfect sphenoid
bone and send it at once to Cambridge? W^m had recently become assistant professor of physiology at
Harvard, and he was attempting to take advantage of
H'ry's yearlong stay in Paris to obtain a particularly
difficult-to-procure item. H'ry did not ask why a pris-
tine specimen of the butterfly-shaped skull bone was
required. He simply made inquiries and set off the
next morning for Maison Vasseur, the very best place
in Paris for such things. M. Vasseur refused the order.
A perfect sphenoid detached from the head was simply
impossible to get, he claimed. Of course, a badly dam-
aged sphenoid might be found at a bric-a-brac shop, but
no perfect sphenoid could ever be purchased separate
from its head. As it happened, M. Vasseur had whole
heads for sale, and he offered H'ry a *"très-belle tête"* for
thirty-five or forty francs. H'ry hesitated, as W^m had
specified the sphenoid only. He decided to report back

and request further instruction. His letter of October 13 drily related his visit to Maison Vasseur, and he apologized for having come up empty-handed. "If you wish it I will instantly purchase & send one," H'ry wrote, meaning an entire head, sphenoid and all.

W^m sent him shopping. H'ry tried again at the establishment of Jules Talrich, but the trip proved a disappointment. "The wretched Talrich" attempted to obtain an independent sphenoid, but discovered in the end that M. Vasseur had been correct. Independent sphenoids could simply not be had. Talrich, too, offered H'ry an entire head, but pointed out that a French head sent across the ocean in a parcel as large as a hat would probably wind up costing more than an American cranium.

W^m's fascination with heads was long-standing. Early in life he had become preoccupied with a photo of a purported death mask of Shakespeare. "It is a superb head," he told H'ry, and he followed up several months later—when H'ry failed to reply—with the insistence that "the mask is extremely interesting." Around the same time, W^m sketched the head of a cadaver in Germany, an image that seemed to project a dark mood he famously suffered in the late 1860s:

And after W^m turned to psychology, he claimed that our sense of self, our "Self of selves," is perceived to consist of motions "in the head or between the head and throat."

"I would give my head to be able to use it," H'ry wrote in 1869, revealing that, for both brothers, interest in heads was merely the beginning of interest in what was happening *inside* the head. "Mysterious & incontrollable (even to one's self)," H'ry wrote four years later, reflecting on his progress as a writer, "is the growth of one's mind." Interest in consciousness mostly ran from older brother to younger. Starting in the late 1870s, with the contract to produce *The Principles of Psychology*, W$^{\underline{m}}$ wrote a series of essays that inched closer and closer to a definitive statement on consciousness. H'ry read each as they appeared. In 1878, "Brute and Human Intellect" cataloged two kinds of thinking, reasoning and narrative, the latter described as "a procession through the mind of groups of images." In 1883, "On Some Omissions in Introspective Psychology" chastised psychological authorities for ignoring the inner life and tried imagery on the problem of thought: "Our mental life, like a bird's life, seems to be made of an alternation of flights and perchings." And several years later, H'ry reported that he had been "fascinated by the *Hidden Self*, in *Scribner*," in which W$^{\underline{m}}$ used a review of Pierre Janet to sneak up on the metaphor that would transcend him: "Our minds are all of them like vessels full of water, and taking in a new drop makes another drop fall out."

By 1890, H'ry admitted that he "quite yearn[ed]" for *The Principles of Psychology*. W$^{\underline{m}}$ ordered his brother a copy two days after the publication date finally arrived. "Most of it is quite unreadable," W^m warned, and steered H'ry toward the "Chapter on Consciousness of Self." W^m had already coined the phrase "stream of consciousness" by then, but the image emerged fully formed only here:

> Consciousness, then, does not appear to itself chopped up in bits. Such words as "chain" or "train" do not describe it fitly as it presents itself in the first instance. It is nothing jointed; it flows. A "river" or a "stream" are the metaphors by which it is most naturally described. *In talking of it hereafter, let us call it the stream of thought, of consciousness, or of subjective life.*

W^m knew that literature had trail-blazed consciousness in more than just the poems of Matthew Arnold. An early "debauch on french fiction," as he described it to H'ry, led him to conclude that "French literature is one long loving commentary on the variations of which individual human nature is capable." The appreciation of variations, of variety, would go on to become a major theme of W^m's career. Whether considering experience, personality types, religion, or truth, the appreciation of variety as a value was central to whatever

18

melioration people could hope to effect. "The notion of the 'one' breeds foreignness," W^m wrote later in life, "and that of the 'many' intimacy."

The problem, he claimed, was that as individual consciousnesses we were all stuck in our heads, stuck in *oneness*. No one could ever truly *know* the mind of another; we were "blind to the feelings of creatures and people different from ourselves." But even this observation had come first from literature. W^m had been particularly struck by Robert Louis Stevenson's essay "The Lantern Bearers" (to H'ry: "The true philosophy is that of Stevenson"), which claimed that "no man lives in the external truth, among salts and acids, but in the warm phantasmagoric chamber of his brain, with the painted windows and the storied walls." W^m quoted pages of the essay in an essay of his own, and concluded that only the "sphere of imagination"—creative work—offered true hope of breaching the membrane that kept us separate and discrete.

Which perhaps explains why W^m had first been drawn to art—and why he was slow in coming around to the science of psychology. "I believe I told you in my last that I had determined to stick to psychology or die," he wrote in 1873. "I have changed my mind." H'ry was saddened at the news. "There seems something half tragic in the tone with which you speak of having averted yourself," he replied. Although the letters sometimes make it seem that H'ry was the source for psychological insight—for example, an 1879 letter in which H'ry hopes W^m's young son will "bloom with dazzling brilliancy" sounds a whole lot like the "blooming, buzzing confusion" W^m used a few years later to describe the consciousness of a child—far more often it's apparent that H'ry slyly mined W^m's work for his fiction.

That H'ry, too, had become preoccupied with consciousness is evident even from his early stories. "A Most Extraordinary Case" (W^m: "read it with much satisfaction") dwells on characters emerging from sleep or experiencing semi-intoxicated states, and the plot of "The Sweetheart of M. Briseux" orbits a painting described as "the picture of a mind, or at least of a mood." H'ry was eternally fascinated by W^m's progress as a psychologist, and he tracked it carefully when he wasn't subtly fostering it. He once asked after a class on physiological psychology that W^m taught, and a few years later he offered heartfelt thanks for a now-lost letter that described a "brain-lecture." For his part,

W^m vacillated in his response to H'ry's fiction. He once praised the "successive psychological steps" in another early story, "Poor Richard" (W^m had read and critiqued an early draft), and in 1888 he claimed there would be no better "delicate national psychologist" than H'ry, should he become one. More often, however, W^m was baffled by H'ry's work. He claimed to read fiction for "refreshment," and while he allowed that the "'*étude*' style of novel" should not be judged by a standard of refreshment, he could not keep himself from chastising his brother. He eventually pleaded with H'ry to avoid "psychological commentaries" entirely.

H'ry did not—and it may be fair to characterize his entire oeuvre as a prolonged project of extending W^m's thinking on consciousness. This can be measured in a number of ways. First, just as W^m entertained "train" and "chain" before settling on "stream" as the best metaphor for thought, so do H'ry's descriptions of consciousness toy with trains and chains before fixing on a wide range of hyperextended water metaphors. (In *The Wings of the Dove*, for instance, thought is portrayed alternately as a "mixture," a "current," a "buoyant medium," etc.) Next, W^m's claim that the frontier of establishing the true nature of human thought

21

belonged to those who in the future would be willing "to adumbrate by at least some possible guess" seems to be met with H'ry's preface to *The Turn of the Screw*, which describes the book's inspiration as "the lively interest of a possible suggestion and process of *adumbration*." H'ry borrowed introspection as well. W^m once wrote that the simple experience of trying to recall a forgotten name revealed the mind's capacity for dual personalities; a few years later, *The Tragic Muse*'s Nick Dormer experiences that very sensation: "He was conscious of a double nature; there were two men in him, quite separate . . . each of whom insisted on having an independent turn at life." And most important, H'ry used W^m's work to understand the creative process. In 1904, H'ry took careful note of a piece that W^m produced on a case of automatic drawing for *Popular Science Monthly*. W^m quoted the drawer at length: "I still think the drawings come from involuntary suggestion, that is, suggestion from the inner mind." Barely seven months later, H'ry produced "The Lesson of Balzac," in which he claimed that the most important thing in fiction, an author's particular "color of air," is "unconsciously suffused" into the work. It "proceeds from the contemplative mind itself."

"The Lesson of Balzac" is perhaps the best example of how H'ry also received lessons from his brother. Just three years earlier, W^{m}'s treatise on religion (H'ry: "I am reading *Varieties of R.E.* with . . . rapturous deliberation") had divvied humanity into two categories of religious potential: the more numerous "healthy-minded folk," who tended to take life uncritically and see good in all things, and the rarer and more mystically minded "sick souls," who struggled to reconcile themselves to a complex world. H'ry retrofitted the bifurcation to a literary community propelled by only "the stiff breeze of the commercial." Just as *The Varieties of Religious Experience* was more interested in unique mystical personalities than common, unblighted folk, so was H'ry less moved by the great morass of popular writers than by the "mystic process" of the more "monkish" Balzac. Even writers of W^{m}'s French debauch received H'ry's cool dismissal. George Sand was "the pride of a sweet-shop." Jane Austen left us "hardly . . . curious of her process." And it was hard "to say where Zola is fine" precisely to the same extent that it was "hard to say where Balzac is . . . not." The problem was that the more popular category of writer, when not crippled by "figures representing . . . ideas," was limited to but a single color of air. Dickens, for example, could give us only the feel of late morning through unwashed windows. George Eliot only the yellowing day as the sun sinks. Balzac, by comparison, had a "greater quantity of 'atmosphere.'" H'ry's measure of Balzac's greatness harkens back to W^m's discrete brains, sadly incapable of knowing each other. The only way we could "know given persons," H'ry wrote, was to see them "from their point of vision, that is from their point of pressing consciousness." Balzac sought not to provide "the *image* of life" but to give life itself, to show "*how* we all are." He achieved this by getting "into the constituted consciousness, into . . . the very skin and bones, of the habited, featured, colored, articulated form of life that he desired to present." And this, in turn, gave us access to Balzac himself. H'ry's description of communicating with Balzac's mind, his consciousness, elaborates on Stevenson's "phantasmagoric chamber of [the] brain":

> We thus walk with him in the great glazed gallery
> of his thought; the long lighted and pictured
> ambulatory where the endless series of windows,
> on one side, hangs over his . . . reinstated garden

of France, and where, on the other, the figures
and the portraits . . . take up position and
expression as he desired.

·4·

A chair in Stevenson's house became known as the
"Henry James chair" in honor of H'ry's frequent vis-
its—which maybe explains why Stevenson escaped
criticism in "The Lesson of Balzac." Or perhaps there
was genuine admiration. In 1888, H'ry claimed that
what was most delightful about Stevenson, like Balzac,
was his "constant variety of experiment." H'ry never
responded to W^m's commentary on "The Lantern
Bearers," but he would have agreed with Stevenson's
claim that the very best storytelling attempted to do
what poetry had always done: sink down into "the
mysterious inwards of psychology" so as to arrive at
the "true realism."

H'ry likened both Balzac and Stevenson to painters—which is telling, in light of the fact that W^m actually *was* a painter. W^m, too, counted writing and painting in the same breath, but he did so in reverse order.

"Your article on Historical novels was very good,"

25

W^m wrote on September 26, 1867, in the same letter in which he attested to his French debauch. He was twenty-five years old, bored in Berlin. He was eating out a lot (he complained that waiters "dressed in cast off wedding suits" were the plague of his life), and he begged H'ry to list his recent reading and to explain a stray comment he'd made about having found no good books of late. H'ry's short piece in the *Nation* had surveyed the territory between history and literature, and discussed works that fell in between. He argued that artistically poor books can nevertheless have instructive historical value and that, by contrast, good books can prove themselves worthless by failing to comport with recognizable truth. The latter was more lamentable. "It is, of course, not well for people of imagination to have the divine faculty constantly snubbed and cross-questioned and held to account . . . but it is very well that it should hold itself responsible to certain uncompromising realities." What realities? W^m may have had an idea, as scarcely a month later it struck him that he might try his hand at reviewing Herman Grimm's latest novel. He had nothing else to do—why not try? He related to H'ry how the work went—"sweating fearfully for three days, erasing, tearing my hair, copying, recopying &c, &c. . . . Style is not my forte"—and he enclosed the finished product such that H'ry might correct it and see it through to publication (which he did). W^m's letter was harder on Grimm than the review had been: "[He has] an extreme belief in the existence and worth of truth . . . [but] a want of careless animal spirits—wh. by the bye seem to be rather characteristics of the rising generation." In other words, Grimm and many others sacrificed vivid depictions of their passionate minds, so like sanctuaries or museums, so as to aspire to the salts and acids, to a rigid objectivity that was both unattainable and unrealistic.

For W^m, the problem harked back to a drama that had played out in art hundreds of years earlier. Six months later—in a letter from Dresden reflecting on Italian painting, a missive at one moment interrupted by a dinner of Kalbsbraten, a performance of Beethoven's *Ninth Symphony*, and a bowl of chocolate—he began to rethink his French debauch. He'd seen quite a bit of art in the meantime, and he was now weighing the damage that tended to result from battling artistic schools. Old masters like José Ribera and Guido Reni surely had talent, he claimed, but to

27

anyone standing "outside of the race course of school-competition" they appeared cold and heartless. Literature had a similar problem. "I've no doubt that the present school of novel-writing, I mean the french realistic school," he wrote H'ry, "will strike people hereafter just as the later Roman & Bolognese pictures strike us." Though earnest, both painters and novelists missed "the one thing needful." They strove after "mere fact, truth of detail," and thereby passed over the "higher and more intellectual harmony" that was evident in the work of the schools' founders, if not their students. W$^{\underline{m}}$ would later import this basic dynamic to religion—something essential was lost in the attempt to transmit the experience of religious mystics to their followers—but for now he ended his treatise with a request that he be excused for his "vague tirade of unripe . . . impressions."

If W$^{\underline{m}}$ was unripe, H'ry was fresh from the vine. No letter from H'ry survives for a year after W$^{\underline{m}}$'s tirade, but he likely would have seen the current crop of realists as secondhand, second-rate inheritors of Balzac, the mystic of French literature and "the father of us all." The brothers' theories on realism would continue to evolve in exhaustive exchanges about George El-

28

iot and George Sand. W^m had mixed feelings about Eliot, considering *Middlemarch* a "blasted artistic failure" but also a "well of wisdom." To his mind, Eliot had the problem of many female writers: they were so surprised to discover that they had *any* faculty to philosophize that they did it until it became tedious. This was so apparent in *Daniel Deronda* that W^m confessed to "a sort of tender pity for the . . . authoress." H'ry liked *Middlemarch* more, though he praised W^m's criticism of it, and he called *Daniel Deronda* "a dead, though amiable failure." He elaborated in the *Atlantic Monthly*, claiming that *Daniel Deronda* lacked "current," and *Romola* "absolutely stagnat[ed]." This captured, to his mind, a basic difference between Eliot and Sand: "George Eliot is solid and George Sand is liquid." If this seemed to aim at streams of consciousness, W^m wasn't buying it. "G.S. babbles her improvisations on," he wrote H'ry, "so that I never begin to believe a word of what she says." He called for demonstrative extracts in whatever H'ry planned to write of Sand, which proved difficult because H'ry found "it impossible to re-read her." He, too, had a hard time believing her, and eventually claimed that she lacked a "method of truth." Her real problem was that she was an "optimist," which, while admirable, put her at odds with the world as it actually stood. "Something even better in a novelist," H'ry wrote, "is that tender appreciation of actuality which makes even the application of a single coat of rose color seem an act of violence."

For H'ry, the search for a better kind of realism had begun long before W$^{\underline{m}}$ sat down to Kalbsbraten in Berlin. The problem must have loomed for him: how could one follow in Balzac's footsteps without diluting him? How could one absorb his lessons without becoming a disciple? His solution was to aim for a realism that remained loyal to more than mere facts and truths of detail, a realism that held true to what was both apparent and poignant: we were all stuck in our skulls, and the world was in nowise better described than as frustrating, confusing, and ambiguous.

Just a week and a half after his tirade, W$^{\underline{m}}$ seemed to glimpse that this was what H'ry was up to. Reacting to "An Extraordinary Life," he offered an admission:

[I] think I may have partly misunderstood your aim heretofore, and that one of the objects you have in view has been to give an impression like that we often get of people in life. Their orbits

come out of space and lay themselves for a short
time along of ours, and *then off they whirl again*
into the unknown, leaving us with little more
than an impression of their reality and a feeling
of baffled curiosity as to the mystery of the
beginning and end of their being.

Emphasis on *"whirl,"* which speaks to the core of the
brothers' similar take on reality and their differences
as to what ought to be done about it.

·5·

"Whirl" returns to Shakespeare, whose influence for
W^{m} stretched all the way back to his very first letter,
and who, for H'ry, was so "immense" that one "need
not press the case of his example." The letters cite
Shakespeare often, without quotation marks, such as
when H'ry, in 1893, complained of an overfull work
schedule and social obligations: "It is again the whirligig of time." That this slightly distorted *Twelfth Night's*
original meaning does not seem to have bothered
W^{m}, who four years later, in complaining of a speaking engagement at a crowded park, hewed closer to

H'ry's meaning: "It's a strange freak of the whirligig of fortune that finds me haranguing the multitude on Boston Common." W$^{\underline{m}}$ had a particular fondness for the word. In 1868, writing to Oliver Wendell Holmes Jr., he claimed that a sadness that had descended upon him was due to ghosts "dancing a senseless whirligig" about him, and in an 1896 essay he claimed that as soon as "the whirligig of time goes round," science would appear shortsighted for having preferred an impersonal worldview to a personal one. H'ry must have taken careful note as "whirligigs" appeared serially in *The Principles of Psychology*, in *The Will to Believe*, in a speech that H'ry praised in 1903 ("your beautiful Harvard address"), and in a plaintive 1905 letter regretting the increasing infrequency of their correspondence: "The wheel of life seems to be whirling for each of us in such wise that we 'don't write.'" A few years later, in *The American Scene*, H'ry set out to prove that he could stretch Shakespeare's metaphor just as easily as he had stretched the stream of consciousness:

> The term I use may appear extravagant, but it was a fact, none the less, that I seemed to take full in my face, on this occasion, the cold stir of air

produced when the whirligig of time has made one of its liveliest turns. It is always going, the whirligig, but its effect is so to blow up the dust that we must wait for it to stop a moment, as it now and then does with a pant of triumph, in order to see what it has been at.

Of the many attempts that have been made to distill the brothers' essential differences, none works quite so simply or succinctly as the snipping away of "gig" from "whirligig." If "whirligig," as a name for a twirling gadget, relies on Cartesian philosophy and characterizes the universe as a simple turning machine susceptible to comprehension and repair, then "whirl" melts the image (for example, "whirlpool"), and proposes that the only true solace comes from renderings of the whirling world whose accuracy makes bearable the turbulence of our own streams. W^{m} clearly preferred the former: when he came round to proposing his grand fix for the problem of truth in philosophy, pragmatism, he defined it, in part, as a "method," echoing the "method of truth" that H'ry had found lacking in George Sand. In preferring the latter, H'ry proposed a different method for a different purpose. He did not aim for a unified theory of truth; rather, adherence to a better, fluid realism—a realism that did not substitute certainty and simplicity for the universe's irreducible spiraling complex ambiguity—is the thread woven through his career: it's the figure in his carpet.

But how exactly should one be a weaver of stories, when storytelling itself, as H'ry noted in "The Lesson of Balzac," tended to organize unruly reality into ruled scenes? H'ry's work proposed multiple solutions. Narrators in H'ry's early stories balk at their own omniscience ("If I were telling my story from Mrs. Mason's point of view . . . I might make a very good thing of the statement that this lady had deliberately and solemnly conferred . . . upon my hero; but I am compelled to let it stand in this simple shape"). His dialogue—maddeningly, for W$^{\underline{m}}$—focused as much on the chaos of actual human speech as it did on clearly conveying the content of the conversations described. W$^{\underline{m}}$ recognized the variety of H'ry's techniques even if he couldn't wholly sign on to them: he lamented the losing of "the story in the sand" at the end of *The Tragic Muse*, but admitted "that is the way things lose themselves in real life." Late in their lives W$^{\underline{m}}$ made special mention of H'ry's preface to *The Wings of the Dove*: it "throws much psychologic light on your creative process." Here, H'ry had acknowledged that his goal in the story of a dying young woman and the small cast of characters caught in the orbit of her demise was to depict the growing, changing consciousness of a girl, but to "approach her circuitously . . . as an unspotted princess is ever dealt with." He was elaborating on the story itself, and the novel's own description of Milly Theale defends his better realism:

> She worked—and seemingly quite without design—upon the sympathy, the curiosity, the fancy of her associates, and we shall really ourselves scarce otherwise come closer to her than by feeling their impression and sharing, if need be, their confusion.

·6·

They often returned to that word—"impression"—in both work and letters.

On April 26, 1869, H'ry began a letter from Oxford that would take him four days to complete. He was replying to a malaise that W^m had been suffering for some time at home, having been laid low by his back and frustrated ambitions. H'ry encouraged him to "spurn the azure demon," and take heart from H'ry's own "adventures." How could W^m do that? H'ry sat down after dinner to record a walk he'd taken earlier in the afternoon. "I feel as if I should like to make a note of certain recent impressions," he wrote, "before they quite fade out of my mind." He proceeded with a story in which he acted as postman, walking through Oxford's colleges to deliver a letter for a friend:

> It was a perfect evening & in the interminable
> British twilight the beauty of the whole place
> came forth with magical power. There are no
> words for these colleges. As I stood last eveg.
> within the precincts of mighty Magdalen,
> gazed at its great serene tower & uncapped my
> throbbing brow in the wild dimness of its courts,
> I thought that the heart of me would crack with
> the fulness of satisfied desire.

The chronicle continues likewise for several pages. The goal of the impressions is to get W^m as close as possible to H'ry's "throbbing brow," and thereby enable him to endure his dark mood. The value of recorded impressions could be applied to art as easily as to strolls, and a few months later, now in Rome, H'ry harkened back to W^m's complaint about Herman Grimm's want of animal spirits in describing his viewing of the paintings of Tintoretto: "I never manage to write but a very small fraction of what has originally occurred to me. What you call the 'animal heat' of contemplation is sure to evaporate within half an hour."

Long before the surviving correspondence begins, W^m and H'ry gestated together in the womb of art, forging their brotherhood in wandering turns through museums in Paris and London. When W^m studied painting in the Newport studio of William Henry Hunt in 1860—at the time, landscape artist John La Farge was the only other student—H'ry tagged along, sometimes dabbling with drawings of his own.

"Your eyes are windows through which you receive impressions," Hunt told them, "keeping yourself as passive as warm wax, instead of being active." This maybe helps to explain why W^m abandoned art; biographers would later describe his personality in childhood as marked by "activity"; he was outgoing and extroverted. H'ry, by way of contrast, was marked by "passivity"; he was quiet, and lived in a "world of 'impressions.'" H'ry had no talent as a painter, yet the time proved formative for him anyway: La Farge, who once painted H'ry's portrait, is credited with introducing H'ry to Balzac and with helping to steer him toward writing with the observation that all the arts are one. (*The Tragic Muse*'s Nick Dormer: "All art is one—remember that, Biddy dear.")

The great truth and task of the universe, as both brothers saw it, now seems to congeal: we are all of us hopelessly awash inside a whipping, whirling, accelerating rush of facts, images, incidents, experiences, all of which buffet up against us, strike us, pound us, *concuss* us, leaving us battered, dented, *impressed and depressed*, until we find a way to usefully surf the whirling current. H'ry was first to fashion a seaworthy vessel in the form of a career, navigating his way to a viable channel long before W^m did. W^m's dark mood of the late 1860s—a crisis that appears thinly disguised as a case study of the "sick soul" in *The Varieties of Religious Experience*—can be attributed to an inability to plot a singular course through a hurricane of impressions.

W^m famously hoisted himself out of his malaise with the work of Charles Renouvier and the decision to believe in free will, but if from there he came to think that a professional voyage into the science of the mind would float him to a more comfortable home, he must have been disappointed. The preeminent philosopher of the mind at the time was Herbert Spencer. In "Brute and Human Intellect," W^m dismissed Spencer's view with a characterization that sounds eerily like Hunt's advice: "[Spencer] regards the creature as absolutely passive clay, upon which 'experience' rains down. The clay will be impressed most deeply where the drops fall thickest, and so the final shape of the mind is moulded." The problem with this was that it ignored the will that saved W$^{\underline{m}}$. It implied that all experiences were the same, which even casual introspection could reject. "My experience is what I agree to attend to," W$^{\underline{m}}$ argued back. "Only those items which I notice shape my mind—without selective interest, experience is an utter chaos." In other words, once you hitch a ride on the stream's conveyor, you have a tool, you have a rudder, and your consciousness is precisely that which scoops logical sequence from sensation's burbling cauldron. In terms of impressions, W$^{\underline{m}}$ took solace in "an admirable passage" from James Martineau: "Experience proceeds and intellect is trained . . . not by reduction of pluralities of impression to one, but by the opening out of one into many."

The early letters are so full of "impressions" they're really rough drafts of essays. Initially, for H'ry—even though he read "Brute and Human Intellect" in 1878—impressions were less a lens through which one could inspect psychology than they were a kind of perishable commodity. H'ry always wrote for money—W$^{\underline{m}}$ frequently fretted over the length of H'ry's letters, given his usual commission—and he worried that his impressions could dry up if he didn't use them quickly enough. In 1886, he complained to W$^{\underline{m}}$ that his impression of Bar Harbour "has grown now too dim" for use. At least in this context, impressions seemed best suited for descriptive travel sketches that were easy to write and paid well. But as early as 1873, H'ry had begun to doubt description ("I doubt whether a year or two hence, I shall have it in me to describe houses and mountains, or even cathedrals & pictures"), and by 1895 he had tired of the process of gathering impressions ("I sometimes feel as if I had already got all the impressions in life I can take in"). By 1901, he seemed disillusioned with description entirely—the problem being, as he saw it, that too often a huge gulf opened between a given description and the thing it described. A few years after moving to Rye, England, H'ry pronounced last rites over description in noting a discrepancy between Thackeray's descriptions of Rye and neighboring Winchelsea and the actual fact of the places: "It is impossible to stand to-day in the high, loose, sunny, haunted square of Winchelsea without wondering what [Thackeray] could have been thinking of. . . . What *could* he—yes—have been thinking of?"

An answer to the problem of description had begun to manifest in H'ry's fiction long before. In 1892, *The Lesson of the Master* (W^m: "Most *perfect* . . . the lesson of the master is a true one") had used impressions to home in on the whirling toil of interior life: "His impression fairly shook him and he throbbed with the excitement of such deep soundings." Even earlier, *The Tragic Muse* (W^m: "With . . . your tragic muse, and . . . my psychology . . . 1890 will be known as the great epocal year in American literature") employed impressions as the currency characters exchanged in fruitless attempts at commerce of minds: "She only watched, in Peter's eyes, for this gentleman's impression of it. That she easily caught, and he measured her impression—her impression of *his* impression—when he went after a few minutes to relieve her." In other words, impressions were no longer things, but thoughts, and the dent of an impression was a better measure of that which had been impressed—of what one had been made to *think*—than it was of whatever hammer had inflicted the blow.

Without quite realizing it, H'ry had returned to art. Of contemporary artists, W^m and H'ry knew and discussed their portraitist and landscape artist friends—Sargent, La Farge, etc.—but they seem to have mostly ignored the avant garde, and the letters never reference Monet, Degas, or Pissarro, the painters whom critic

Edmond Duranty labeled "Impressionists" in 1874. Nevertheless, the letters occasionally aspire to recognizably impressionistic atmospheres. Also in 1874, H'ry scribbled out a notably painterly view of Florence:

> To day is a raw, rainy Sunday of anything but
> an exhilarating kind. The Piazza di Sta Maria
> Novella, before my windows is a wide glittering
> floor, with here and there two legs picking their
> steps beneath an umbrella.

W^m and H'ry never truly left the womb of art, and even the very last letter of the correspondence, from August 1910, details H'ry's purchase of a landscape for W^m's home in Cambridge. Even more telling, H'ry had just a year earlier giddily passed along a review of the recently released New York edition of his collected novels. It was rare for H'ry to agree with a critic.

"This strict fusion of material with form is Mr. James's point of departure," the critic wrote. "He is in the truest sense of the word an impressionist."

In February 1874—just a few months before H'ry waxed impressionistically from his Florentine window—W^m and H'ry had traveled in Italy together. One day, W^m visited Venice's Galleria dell'Accademia and sat for a long time before Titian's *Presentation of the Virgin in the Temple*. The museum was quite chilly, but W^m stayed long enough to share at least an hour's study of the work with an intently interested English couple. He noted the pair as they drew near one another to exchange impassioned impressions of the depicted figures. When W^m was finally chased from the room by the cold, he made a point of sneaking close to eavesdrop for a moment. "What a *deprecatory* expression her face wears!" the woman murmured. "What self-abne*gation!* How *unworthy* she feels of the honour she is receiving!"

Hogwash! W^m thought. Old Titian would have been made sick by such a reaction! For W^m, the English couple feebly attempting to exert an aesthetic sense was a clear demonstration of what could go wrong when human emotions didn't work quite correctly. Nine years later, he sketched the scene in "What Is an Emotion?," an article published in *Mind*, so as to

contrast the couple with "experts and masters" whose reaction to art, long before any emotion kicked in, was determined by a more profound sense of *rightness*. It was only *"Crétins* and Philistines," W^m wrote, who erred by opting for mere "flush and thrill."

H'ry's reaction to W^m on this point is difficult to gauge. He begged off reading "What Is an Emotion?" when it appeared, claiming to have "attacked" the piece only to be "defeated" by it. "I can't give [it] just now the *necessary* time," he wrote. (Somewhat sneakily, he did call W^m's attention to a critical notice of the article; the critic enjoyed W^m's informal style, but warned that unless W^m took care "his readers will begin to suspect that the sober quest of truth is in his case apt to be disturbed by too keen an impulse towards literary effect.")

Perhaps H'ry didn't have time for "What Is an Emotion?" because he recalled that his *own* reactions to art had a few years back come to play a role in "Brute and Human Intellect." Here, W$^{\underline{m}}$ had taken note that in ethical, psychological, and aesthetic matters, "to give a clear reason for one's judgment is a . . . mark of rare genius." But what, he asked, of the preponderance of moments in which clear reason eludes us? The most obvious case of this was "uneducated people." Stop the "first Irish girl" you come across in the street in America, he claimed, and you'll find that she can't even tell you why she prefers this continent to her own. And she was hardly alone. H'ry was there with her, in fact. W$^{\underline{m}}$ called on H'ry's letters from Italy, the same letters in which H'ry attempted to articulate his impressions of Tintoretto, Titian, Veronese, and others, to illustrate the breadth of the problem: "But if you ask your most educated friend why he prefers Titian to Paul Veronese, you will hardly get more of a reply."

H'ry's Italian letters came from the same trip during which he suffered his "moving intestinal drama," though by the time he'd made it to Rome he had found a pill that worked. ("I needn't dilate upon it," he wrote home, happy to move on to other subjects.) H'ry certainly recognized the difficulty of fully articulating impressions. "Alack! 'tis poor work talking of them," he wrote of his reaction to a range of pieces by Michelangelo. He seemed to think that whatever fleeting views one had were best described with streams of consciousness: "On the spot my intellect gushed forth a torrent of wisdom & eloquence," he wrote of his final visit to the *Moses*, "but where is that torrent now?"

At the time, W^m seemed to agree that a certain gushing unruliness was perhaps the best we could hope for in turning raw impressions into language:

> I can well sympathize with what must be the
> turmoil of your feeling before all this wealth—
> that strange impulse to exorcise it by extracting
> the soul of it and throwing it off *in words*—which
> translation is in the nature of things impossible.

For H'ry, this must have stung a little, at least in retrospect, for it didn't particularly jibe with having his impressions likened, a few years later, to those of a naive Irish lass. Something had changed. The brothers' aesthetics had begun to diverge. W^m had come to conclude that the ability to state clear reasons for one's thinking was the mark of genius; H'ry had grown only firmer in his belief that we need never attempt anything other than the slicing open of our veins to let the impressions flow. It's precisely because W$^{\underline{m}}$ and H'ry gestated together in the womb of art that their evolving theoretical differences first made themselves apparent in opinions of art. The broader truth was perhaps even painful. W$^{\underline{m}}$ had once had the hand of a painter, but always lacked the soul of one; H'ry, precisely the opposite.

H'ry recognized this early, and he came to realize that if he couldn't be a painter himself then what he needed to do was figure out how to *use* art. In 1869, defending what appeared to his family as a wasteful vacation in Europe, H'ry explained that his goal was to "lay the basis of a serious interest in art . . . which may be of future use to me." The following year, he identified the art of Florence in particular as a "prompter or inspirer of some sort," leading him not toward an assessment of its history, but to its employ as an "irradiating focus of light on some other matter." He first linked painting with literature through Titian, who reminded him of Shakespeare: "He belongs to the same family and produces very much the same effect." Serially applying W$^{\underline{m}}$'s argument on truth of detail, his view evolved as he shifted from artist to artist. Tintoretto was notable because he first "strike[s] you as the poorest & ends by impressing you as the greatest of colorists." Michelangelo was "so far from perfection, so finite, so full of errors," yet the *Moses* produced "a great sensation—the greatest a work can give." H'ry was already headed for his better realism, but could conceive of no explanation for it yet. Of Tintoretto, he admitted to W$^{\underline{m}}$, "I should be sadly at a loss to make you understand in what his great power consists." But it hardly mattered that he might never find words for it: "I'd give a great deal to be able to fling down a dozen of his pictures into prose of corresponding force & color."

Art provided both process and plot points. In 1895, H'ry remarked on a James family scandal that erupted over a likeness W$^{\underline{m}}$ once produced of a beloved cousin, and H'ry's stories often exploit similar tensions: family dramas resulting from the painting of a portrait or from the choice to dedicate one's life to art rather than marriage. He was right that his idle journey through Europe would equip him with a lifetime's supply of impressions. His Italy letters—once shared with Emerson, who was so keen on them he wanted to borrow them for study; Henry Sr. refused—were a kind of mortar poured into the divots each artist left behind. H'ry was left with a shelf of molds forever in easy reach. *The Tragic Muse*'s Peter Sherringham reminds Bridget Dormer "of a Titian," and Nick Dormer later feels an ineffectual longing to have "a go" at Titian and Tintoretto. *The Wings of the Dove*'s Susan Shepherd recognizes that the story's advancing intrigue has become "a Veronese picture, as near as can be." In both novels, art betrays consciousness: Miriam Rooth is "apt to drop" particular observations while "under the suggestion" of Titian or Bronzino, and Milly Theale speaks at one moment of her mysterious illness "almost as if under [the] suggestion" of a Bronzino, and at another finds herself surrounded by Turners and Titians at London's National Gallery, which seem to "[join] hands" about her and trigger an ensuing reverie.

·8·

This last description seems almost to cite a plaintive remark W^m once made to H'ry as his career trajectory in science and academia began to take shape. Painting was slipping farther and farther away:

But I envy ye the world of Art. Away from
it . . . we sink into a flatter blanker kind of
consciousness, and indulge in an ostrichlike
forgetfulness of all our richest potentialities—and
they startle us now and then when by accident
some rich human product, pictorial, literary, or
architectural slaps us with its tail.

W^m had always approached art more academically
than H'ry, comparing works so as to plot the arc of
art history, attempting to gauge whether it was the
Germans or the Venetians who were the true brothers of Greeks, etc. In 1882, he planned an essay that
would apply natural selection to competing schools
of art—artistic Darwinism—but never executed it. By
the time of the writing of *The Principles of Psychology*, art
had receded completely, becoming less overt subject
matter than convenient metaphor. "This chapter is like
a painter's first charcoal sketch upon his canvas," he
wrote at the start of "The Stream of Consciousness."
A field of grass might *appear* green, he allowed a short
time later, describing the complexity of subjective sensation, "yet a painter would have to paint one part of

it dark brown, another part bright yellow, to give it its real sensational effect."

That art faded into W^m's background just as it climbed into H'ry's foreground expressed figuratively what had once been expressed literally. In 1869, W^m offered H'ry invaluable criticism in response to a long, early story. "Gabrielle de Bergerac" employs a now-familiar Jamesian tool: a foreground "frame tale" in which a character somehow bequeaths a story to a notably H'ry-like narrator, and a background tale that is repeated for the reader. W^m objected to the ending of "Gabrielle de Bergerac," which after a long dip into a background drama returns briefly to the foreground frame tale. "Very exquisitely touched," W^m wrote, "but the denouement bad in that it did not end with Coquelin's death. . . . The end is both humdrum and improbable." What he meant was that the story could remain asymmetrical. H'ry didn't need to return to the foreground—the story could simply fade into its background and end there. As it happened, the interest of backgrounds was a subject actually described in the background story of "Gabrielle de Bergerac": a character recalls Gustave Doré's illustrations of Charles Perrault's *Sleeping Beauty*, in particular an image in

52

which three shadowed foreground figures gesture off to a foggy but better lit castle in the distance. It was the light *and* the vagueness, the story claimed, that drew the eye to the rear of the image and triggered the working of the mind:

> What does the castle contain? What secret is locked in its stately walls? What revel is enacted in its long saloons? What strange figures stand aloof from its vacant windows? You ask the question, and the answer is a long revery.

For H'ry, the castle was like the citadel of consciousness forever running in the background of human intercourse; it was the more compelling tale whirling *be-hind* whatever simple plots storytellers strung clumsily together. H'ry carefully applied W^m's advice whenever he employed the foreground frame tale in the future, most notably in *The Turn of the Screw*, which ends the harrowing account of the governess's haunting with the dramatic death of a child, and never returns to the circle of friends who are listening to the story read aloud around a Christmas fire.

While H'ry clearly benefited from W^m's advice, it's not at all clear that W^m understood *how* his advice had become useful. Outside of stories, he wanted *nothing* left in the background. This was made apparent in 1869, when W^m wrote to H'ry of visiting John La Farge to view several paintings then still under way. One in particular, *Paradise Valley*, a broad image of green fields near Newport, absolutely frayed W^m's nerves. The painting had begun with a large female figure situated in the foreground, a white-draped presence occupying almost two-thirds of the large canvas.

Sometime during the work on the piece, La Farge had been moved to paint over the figure completely, leaving only the background and a tiny baby sheep. W^m couldn't get his head around it. He understood

the landscape, which was "as big as all out doors and
flooded with light even in its botchy state." But he
couldn't begin to fathom why La Farge had eliminated
the woman in the foreground. "He ought to repaint
a figure in it no matter how 'quaint' it will look to the
vulgar."

They had begun to disagree even about what it meant to be "vulgar."

H'ry took his cue from Balzac. *Eugenie Grandet*'s eponymous heroine, for example, comes from "a class of females found in the middle ranks of life, whose beauty appears vulgar." But Eugenie is not vulgar herself: "There was nothing *pretty* about Eugenie; she was beautiful with that beauty so easily overlooked, and which the artist alone catches." H'ry spent a lifetime trying to apply a similar principle to language. In "The Question of Our Speech" (an address first delivered in 1905 to an audience of "*5, or 6 hundred* people" in Philadelphia) he warned of the "vulgarization" resulting from "common schools and the 'daily paper,'" and suggested that "avoiding vulgarity, arriving at lucidity" was an art to be cultivated if we hoped to distinguish our speech from "the barking or the roaring of animals."

In other words, to be vulgar was to be less obscene than obvious. For W$^{\underline{m}}$, it had always meant something slightly different. His pained work on the style of his Grimm review had struck him as a balancing act between "pomposity & vulgar familiarity." He allowed

56

that style meant leaving the essential unspoken—of Turgenev, he wrote in one letter, "[He] has a sense of worlds within worlds whose existence is unsuspected by the vulgar"—but he also equated it with the careless redundancy of writers who fetishized an offhand air. In 1883, W^{m} fretted over "the determination on the part of all who write now to do it as amateurs, & never use the airs & language of a professional, to be first of all a layman & a gentleman, & to pretend that your ideas came to you accidentally." A decade and a half earlier, he had criticized H'ry's stories for giving "a certain impression of the author clinging to his gentlemanliness tho' all else be lost."

Which was actually prescient. By the late 1880s, H'ry had begun to tire of fiction; drawn by the financial lure of the theater, he had begun dabbling as a playwright. The public aspect of the experiment discomfited him from the start. "There wd. be much good for me to tell you of my Play & its successors if I were to speak of the business in any way," he wrote in June 1890. "But I must not, for awfully good reasons, & I beseech you not to either." It wasn't that he was afraid; it was that there was decorum to consider. The next month, he calmly accepted the lackluster performance of his most recent novel. A writer couldn't concern himself with "popularity," he wrote. One "must go one's way & know what one's about" and understand that it was popularity enough if a work made any "audible vibration." A few months later, however, he could barely contain his excitement over the preparations for the opening of his stage adaptation of *The American.* He apologized for his "vulgarities" in this regard; he happily related details of rehearsals, of venue, and of future plays that might also be put into production. He had a "kind of mystic confidence in the ultimate life of the piece," and claimed he had always known that plays were the genre to which his work was most suited. Critics disagreed; *The American* was panned. The show ran only sixty-nine nights; H'ry made no profit from it.

"TELL THIS TO NO ONE," he told W^m.

He kept at it, frustrating as it was. Over the next few years, he changed producers and suffered through endless strings of setbacks and delays. H'ry wasn't used to working with others. "They simply kicked me . . . out of the theatre," he wrote in 1894. "How can one rehearse with people who are dying to get rid of you?" H'ry hadn't even employed a literary agent for the first fifteen years of his career. "I can *meet* these horrors, in a word, I think (for another year)," he wrote finally, "but I can't *talk* about them."

W^m valiantly resisted the urge to remind H'ry that he had offered him fair warning. Back when H'ry first showed interest in the theater, W^m related a story of stumbling across a street poster advertising the attractions of a play soon to open: "NO PLOT—ALL FUN!" "What a relief to the intellect to have *no* plot!" W^m wrote. His point was that in writing for the stage one needed to remain vigilant to "the qualities that the stage requires." He advised H'ry to "cold bloodedly throw in enough *action* to please the people." In 1894, W^m invited several friends to his summerhouse in New Hampshire to read through several of H'ry's plays as a group. They were received, W^m was forced to admit, "with a certain tinge of disappointment." The problem of one was that "the *matter* [was] so slight." In another, a character failed to "show her inside nature enough." In general, the group of readers was left with "a curious unsympathetic and uncanny impression." H'ry's only reply was to suggest that he'd done his best to make his works "artful & very human."

In January 1895, W^m reported that he and his wife, Alice, in Boston, "prayed on the bended knees of [their] souls" all day long for the telegram that would herald the success of *Guy Domville*'s opening night in London. It never arrived. Two days later, W^m wrote to say that while he could not imagine the play having failed completely, he could "conceive of a lack of flagrant success." H'ry had been licking his wounds. The play had done more than flop. After the curtain had fallen, a raucous display of malice had erupted from the gallery, and the ensuing scene, a quarter of an hour in which H'ry's friends close to the stage attempted to applaud over the hoots and jeers of callous roughs in the shadows—a spectacle that culminated with the play's nervous director appearing on stage to quickly apologize for the production—is one of the better documented episodes in the many biographies of H'ry's life. What's worth revisiting is the way he described it once he mustered the courage to put it all in a letter.

The play had never really had a chance, he wrote. His "extremely human" effort was met by a mob that responded with "*roars* (like those of a cage of beasts at some infernal 'Zoo')." The problem was really twofold. First, the play, which he had striven to make as clear and transparent as possible, simply flew "over the heads of the *usual* vulgar theatre going London public." They did not want plays of "different *kinds*," H'ry wrote, only productions that their clumsy vision recognized as similar to what they'd seen before. Second, the critics had been "ill-natured & densely stupid & vulgar." Together they amounted to a "squalid crew," but one in particular was "awfully vulgar & Philistine." The second night had gone better than the first, but H'ry feared the play would be withdrawn. He was right. *Guy Domville* closed after thirty-two nights, and was replaced by Oscar Wilde's *The Importance of Being Earnest.* In the end, H'ry was left with "horror for the abysmal vulgarity & brutality of the theatre."

·10·

What W$^{\underline{m}}$ would have recognized from this was that H'ry's reaction to his vulgar audience was in itself a vulgar act—or would have been had he shared his impressions with anyone else. More important, H'ry's precise problem was that the vulgar taste of his audience matched perfectly the vulgar aesthetic that W$^{\underline{m}}$ attempted to prescribe for La Farge's *Paradise Valley.* The unavoidable suggestion would have been that W$^{\underline{m}}$ himself was vulgar.

In reply, W^m showed restraint. By that time, the brothers' home lives had diverged even more than their philosophies: W^m now had four children; H'ry had never married. As W^m had labored to establish a family and inch his way into an academic career, he watched as his younger brother jetted straight into the heart of the world's literary elite. (Whenever W^m suggested that home life and teaching kept him from his true labor, H'ry noted that it must be nice to have a wife to handle household duties, and claimed that he longed for a steady position that would leave him free to produce only "a small amount of 1st class work.")

As late as 1887, W^m confessed to anxiety over the pace of his own progress: "A strange coldness has come over me with reference to all my deeds and productions. . . . [E]verything I've done and shall do seems so *small*." H'ry offered assurances ("You will live to do great things yet"), but they must have rung hollow. In 1885, W^m noted that H'ry's work was already so popular that Harvard students had overemployed it as subject matter for an annual essay test; H'ry had been placed on a list of forbidden topics. By 1895, W^m did have a successful book of his own, but the twelve years it had taken to write paled by comparison to H'ry's heavy, steady output. In one month alone—June 1893—H'ry published a novel and two volumes of essays.

A lack of tangible reward is probably what W$^{\underline{m}}$ was missing when, in 1891, he wrote to H'ry, "All intellectual work is the same—the artist feeds the public on his own bleeding insides." He went on to describe a reading he had recently given, the initial delivery of "The Moral Philosopher and the Moral Life," presented to 100 members of the Yale Philosophy Club. The room remained mute throughout the address, and his host mentioned the talk not at all on their walk home. "Apparently, it was unmentionable," W$^{\underline{m}}$ wrote. But W$^{\underline{m}}$ had a better sense of humor about such things than H'ry. "Speaking of the unmentionable," he continued, and went on to joyfully gossip about an obscenity trial then under way in Boston.

W$^{\underline{m}}$ both doted on and teased H'ry. In 1902, *The Wings of the Dove* set the stage for the latter. Near the start of the book, the novel's principal couple is introduced at a party. Kate Croy's vivid memory of the portentous meeting is shot through with the quiet, thrilling impropriety of breeched boundaries:

Kate afterwards imaged to herself . . . a ladder against a garden wall, and had trusted herself so to climb it as to be able to see over into the probable garden on the other side. On reaching the top she had found herself face to face with a gentleman engaged in a like calculation at the same moment, and the two inquirers had remained confronted on their ladders. The great point was that for the rest of the evening they had been perched—they had not climbed down.

W^m was just as befuddled by *The Wings of the Dove* as he had been by *Paradise Valley*. When the book first appeared, he claimed that H'ry had "reversed every traditional canon of story-telling (especially the fundamental one of *telling* the story)." It was now seven years later, but he must have feared the theatrical debacle all over again, and he wondered whether the difficulty of H'ry's writing was "fatal and inevitable" or "deliberate." The book got under his skin—"I went fizzling about concerning it"—and he was still striving to understand it as late as 1909. Before then, however, he found a way to illustrate an essential point about both the book and his brother's life.

Back in 1899, W^m called H'ry's attention to "The Gospel of Relaxation," one of three essays W^m had decided to include at the end of *Talks to Teachers*. Here, W^m quoted a Scottish doctor who claimed that Americans wore "too much expression on [their] faces"; he suggested they "tone [them]selves down." W^m disagreed, of course, and lashed out in turn at the codfish eyes and the "slow, inanimate demeanor" of all from the British Isles. What he surely wanted H'ry to note, however, was his claim that "Americans who stay in Europe long enough" wind up thinking and acting more like the Scottish doctor than they do their brethren. H'ry had been living in England for two decades by then.

Eight years later, having more or less continuously fretted over *The Wings of the Dove*, W^m was invited to England to deliver the lectures that would become *A Pluralistic Universe*. He had gone a long way toward catching up to his brother by then. He had not published his first book until he was forty-eight, but his reputation had grown steadily thereafter, and in recent years he had become a very popular traveling speaker. In 1901–1902, he delivered Scotland's Gifford lectures, which in book form became *The Varieties of Religious*

Experience, a best seller. The new appointment enabled him to again visit H'ry in Rye. As it happened, Lamb House had a garden, and the garden's stone wall separated H'ry's property from the grounds of a famous inn. W^m had heard a rumor that G. K. Chesterton, whom he had never met but suspected as a sympathizer to W^m's even more recent *Pragmatism*, was then a guest. One day in H'ry's garden, W^m struck on an idea: just as Kate Croy had deliciously imagined the initial meeting of her love, he seized a handy ladder and placed it against the stone wall so as to climb to the top and peer over in an attempt to spot Chesterton. But for H'ry, what was permissible for a fictional character's inner life was vulgar in reality. It was simply not done in England, he objected. The brothers argued, and when H. G. Wells happened to drive up a short time later he found H'ry in such an agitated state that he separated the two. W^m went off with Wells willingly; his point had been made. H'ry forbade for himself in real life—indeed, counted them as vulgar—precisely those things that gave it zest.

A similar issue had cropped up a few years earlier, as the brothers planned the trip together through the United States that H'ry would use to produce *The Amer-*

ican Scene. The journey's initial outline triggered W^m's protective reflex. He worried over the "désagréments" that the trip would subject H'ry to, the "physical loathing" that certain American manners would inspire. Of particular concern was a practice that made even W^m contemplate expatriation. Whether in hotels or on trains, whenever W^m traveled he found himself confronted with the sight of his fellow Americans happily slurping butter-drenched boiled eggs from cups! He admitted that his reaction to this might be irrational, but the only thing worse to imagine than his own intestinal disgust at such a scene was the sickening tectonic quakes that would surely split H'ry's fragile gut.

Nonsense! H'ry replied. W^m completely misunderstood his motives. Impressions, even of the vulgar, were precisely what he hoped to absorb and digest. To gobble up whatever impressions there were to be had was precisely the point of the entire excursion. Should he shrink from "the one chance that remains . . . in life of anything that can be called a *movement*?" No. He must seek to convert, through observation, imagination, and reflection, even shocking experiences "into vivid and solid *material*."

What you say of the Eggs(!!!) . . . is utterly beside the mark—it being absolutely *for* all that class of phenomena, and every other class, that I nurse my infatuation. I want to see them, I want to see everything.

W$^{\underline{m}}$ duly apologized. "I thought I ought to proffer the thought of 'eggs' and other shocks," he explained, "so that when they came I might be able to say that you went not unwarned."

The American Scene is a peculiar book. In keeping with H'ry's aversion to straightforward travelogue, the account of the journey is less an attempt to chronicle the place through impressions of mountains and railroads and churches and farms than a contemplative survey of the American spirit. In addition to the book, H'ry used the trip with W$^{\underline{m}}$ to produce a series of long articles for *Harper's Bazaar.* Here he revealed that, for him, the consumption of American eggs was far less shocking than the speech of American girls.

"It was a scant impression, no doubt, yet a prompt and a suggestive," the series began, "that I gathered, of a bright fresh afternoon early in October, in the course of a run from Boston down to the further South

Shore." Not long into the journey, H'ry reported, the train stopped for a "bevy" of young girls who climbed aboard and took "vociferous possession" of the car. Ranging in age from fourteen to sixteen, the girls called, giggled, shouted, and romped up and down the aisle, behaving as if they were on a playground. H'ry was scandalized. The first surprising thing was that the girls were all well dressed. There was "nothing of the vulgar in their facial type or their equipment." So how could they behave such? he wondered. Even more surprising, how could it be that the others in the car remained, as they did, wholly indifferent to the scene?

W^m sometimes appears as a "friend" in the *Harper's Bazaar* pieces, offering commentary on American etiquette. But if he was on the train ride he was among those who found the scene unremarkable and, apparently, not vulgar. H'ry, by contrast, was awestruck, for it was "in the manners of the women that the social record writes itself . . . finest." In other words, the scene was a barometer. The manners of American women measured both the ongoing disintegration of polite society and the schism that now separated him from his brother.

H'ry had better relationships with women in his fiction than in real life. The letters, however, offer no refuge to the cauldrons of ink that have been spilled by critical covens endlessly toiling over the brew of H'ry's sexual orientation. Even on the subject of Wilde's imprisonment, H'ry lets slip nothing to W$^{\underline{m}}$—the audience to whom he slipped *everything* else. The letters, in fact, upend the usual thought on *both* brothers' attitudes toward girls and women.

It's generally held that W$^{\underline{m}}$ and H'ry's young cousin Minny Temple, a vivacious girl who moved with her family onto the same street as the Jameses in 1861, was an early romantic interest of W$^{\underline{m}}$'s and served as a model for many of H'ry's heroines. Both brothers have been said to have been in love with Minny, and the girl's death from tuberculosis in 1870 has served as a convenient biographical marker denoting the brothers' passage into adulthood—convenient even for H'ry, who said as much in a memoir in 1913. The letters, however, confound too simplistic a take on Minny's role in the brothers' lives.

On December 5, 1869, just a few months before

70

Minny died, W^m wrote to say that even though he enjoyed her company now, he was conscious of having nourished "unsympathetic hostility" to Minny. He recalled "abusing her" to H'ry the winter before. H'ry noted this only casually, refraining from comment until Minny died. On March 29, 1870, he claimed that it took him only a few hours to reconcile himself to the news. His letter indulges in playful, idiomatic glee in characterizing her—Minny was "a mere subject without an object"; "she has 'gone abroad' in another sense!"—even as it claims that it is too soon to pretend to feel her death. W^m wrote back a few weeks later. The period corresponds with his dark mood, but Minny is not his reply's first order of business, nor does it attribute his "slough" to her death. W^m offers quick thanks for H'ry's letters about Minny—some were not preserved—and then he writes several pages about a water cure that H'ry might pursue in London.

In other words, Minny is less interesting as a nugget of biography than as a literary symbol. Even H'ry recognized this. "She seems a sort of experiment of nature," he wrote. "An attempt, a specimen or example." Too exclusive a biographical focus on Minny undermines the impact other women had on W^m and H'ry:

their sister, Alice; George Eliot and George Sand; and much later, a range of younger friends and cousins.

The subject of women is the best possible lens to use so as to refract the brothers' mutual influence. H'ry's *The Bostonians*, about a mystic of the women's suffrage movement, was written in the wake of a pair of reviews W^m^ produced of women's suffrage books. "*Cut out* and send me your articles in the N[orth]. A[merican]. R[eview].," H'ry had demanded. "Brute and Human Intellect," published just before H'ry wrote *Washington Square* and *The Portrait of a Lady*, ends with a description of the minds of "young wom[e]n of twenty," the classic age of H'ry's heroines. It ran the other way as well. A piece H'ry published on George Sand in 1876—which W^m^ had suggested he write—contains the basic thesis of *Pragmatism*: "Women, we are told, do not value the truth for its own sake, but only for some personal use they make of it." And H'ry's "The Altar of the Dead" (W^m^: "*Exquisite* in tone and texture") claimed that "women have more of the spirit of religion than men" just at that moment when W^m^ was lecturing to large audiences of teachers—mostly women—and had turned his attention toward *The Varieties of Religious Experience*.

H'ry's experimentation with female characters was one of the few aspects of his work that W$^{\underline{m}}$ praised from the start. In 1868, in an otherwise quite critical letter, W$^{\underline{m}}$ wrote, "Your young women seem to me all along to have been done in a very clean manner—they feel like women to me, and have always that atmosphere of loveliness and unapproachability, which the civilized woman wears into the world." H'ry agreed. Nothing drew the imagination like a mysterious young woman. *The Bostonians* focused on precisely those actions of Verena Tarrant that "deepened the ambiguity of her position." Julia Dallow in *The Tragic Muse* exhibited a "perfect uncertainty." In 1880, H'ry even shrugged off some of W$^{\underline{m}}$'s praise: "The young man in *Washington Square* is not a portrait—he is sketched from the outside merely. . . . The only good thing in the story is the girl."

Yet what worked in his fiction plagued him in life. That same year, H'ry was approached in Venice (he often served as host to traveling New Englanders) by the family of poet and transcendentalist Christopher Cranch. H'ry worried over the Cranches' daughter, Carrie, who seemed not inclined to go out much. He saw her on four or five occasions, taking her to museums two or three times. Several years later, Carrie Cranch approached W$^{\underline{m}}$ in America. H'ry was forced to explain. The young woman had gone insane, H'ry said, and the suggestion he seemed to want to refute was that it was all a result of her love for him. "Her insanity connecting itself with me must be pure accident," he wrote. He offered no sympathy. "I hope she may die—it will be the best thing for her. But she probably won't." A year later, he was nonplussed at the news that Carrie Cranch was now in an asylum. She had written again to W$^{\underline{m}}$, to retrieve "little things" of hers that she claimed H'ry had kept in his possession. "Pure hallucination," H'ry wrote.

Carrie Cranch was an extreme case, but after he achieved fame H'ry was stricken with an outbreak of women who wanted to be thought of as the model for his archetypal American girl. In 1904, he fended off rumors that he was engaged to a woman from Kentucky who was both a millionaire and the original Milly Theale. In 1905, there was a stir at the suggestion that the real Daisy Miller had attended one of his lectures. H'ry insisted there was no real Daisy Miller, and the incidents may explain why he wound up attributing so much to Minny Temple. On more than one occasion, either to layer in ironic nuance or to avoid any sense of slander or scandal, H'ry attributed stories or characters to persons already dead.

"Nothing in America," H'ry wrote in his *Harper's Bazaar* series, "more frequently conduces to interest, for the taker of social notes, than the question of the presumable 'social standing' of the flourishing female young." In other words, girls were perfect for stories. Girls moved from the background of society to its foreground on becoming women, and while yet in the shadows, lurking and unclear, they drew the imagination. They certainly drew W^m's, and his biographers have tended to saddle him with a borderline pernicious preoccupation with young women. But his interest is better understood as kin to his disagreement with H'ry over manners. He *liked* American girls who exhibited a kind of "bottled-lightning," he wrote in "The Gospel of Relaxation." It was a phrase he'd once applied to his sister; now, he labeled it an "American ideal." The whole problem with Europe, he claimed, was that Europeans were so wrapped up in stodginess there were "no bottled-lightning girls [to be] found."

The letters document W^m's efforts to get as close as possible to America's dense population of bottled-lightning girls. "Pauline is the best girl I know in this low world," W$^{\underline{m}}$ wrote in 1899, at age fifty-seven. He had met Pauline Goldmark and her four sisters while lecturing at Bryn Mawr, and on a camping trip in the Keene valley in the summer of 1898, "racing with those greyhounds of Goldmarks," he had strained his heart. (The damage never healed, but that didn't stop him from advising H'ry to "make up" to the girls if he had a chance during their European tour.) Even more telling was W$^{\underline{m}}$ and H'ry's prolonged interest in two young cousins, Rosina and Bay Emmet. In 1895, W$^{\underline{m}}$ described Rosina as "much the type of Minny," but with literary ambitions. H'ry's interest was piqued, but he found himself more drawn to Bay, a painter. It wasn't the girls' youth that made them interesting—it was that they were different from most people. Rosina, W$^{\underline{m}}$ wrote, had a great capacity for seeing truth. Bay, H'ry thought, was a "pure" painter, and would continue to improve, but only if she didn't marry. Through to the end of W$^{\underline{m}}$'s life, the brothers kept careful tabs on Rosina and Bay, housing them when they could, cheering their initial employment, and becoming distressed when news of the girls was hard to come by. They showed more interest in Rosina and Bay than they did in W^m's children—or anyone else. There were two reasons for this. On the one hand, W^m and H'ry knew that the pressures of society—gossip—could chase young women into unhappy marriages. On the other, they saw likenesses of themselves in the young aspiring writer and the young aspiring painter.

"No one we meet nowadays," W^m wrote in 1897, when Rosina and Bay finally paid H'ry a visit, "can remind us of *our* youth and its artistic fermentations so much as the clatter of those tongues." For W^m, the girls perhaps recalled the path in life he didn't, or couldn't, choose. Rosina, he wrote in 1907, was a "healthy-minded type"; he had long since described himself as a sick soul. H'ry certainly saw himself in Bay—he noted that her portraits of men were better than her women, just as his own female characters were more convincing than his men. It's tempting to substitute Rosina and Bay for Minny Temple as H'ry's primary model—the girls, after all, came to Europe not long before he embarked on *The Wings of the Dove.* But even that's a simplification, as the very start of the novel sounds less like Minny or Rosina or Bay than like the James childhood home with W^m and H'ry in gender reversal: "Her father's life, her sister's, her own, that of her two lost brothers—the whole history of their house had the effect of some fine florid, voluminous phrase."

"Our relatives don't seem to like us," W^m wrote to H'ry in 1895, in a letter with an attached request for money from one of their male siblings. Wilky and Bob were the family's "lost brothers," and the advantages W^m and H'ry had received (they were kept from the Civil War, by either illness or paternal decree, while Wilky and Bob served), and the success that resulted from those advantages, strained filial relations. Wilky died young, having been expunged from Henry Sr.'s will; Bob sank into alcoholism and was eventually regarded as an annoyance. What W^m really meant was that *male* relatives didn't seem to like them.

In 1907, just two weeks after W^m read H'ry's *Harper's Bazaar* series, he wrote concerning a "matter of charity." Mary James, the daughter of a cousin, Howard—a rakish man who had once descended drunk on H'ry's London apartment while H'ry was away and raised such a fuss that one of the servants had an epileptic fit—was in need of assistance. Mary was "diff^t in disposition" from her father and siblings, W^m claimed. Plus, she was a widow with child. "For some years past," W^m

wrote, "[she] has made her living mostly by standing as model in wholesale 'Cloak stores' to show styles to 'buyers'—a deplorable pursuit." Was it not their duty to protect her from gossip and "lift her up"? Could H'ry contribute $100 for instruction in stenography? "It's impossible *not* to," H'ry replied, enclosing a check.

They were too late; the money went unspent. The young woman had married.

·12·

H'ry's preface to 1888's *The Reverberator* (W<u>m</u>: "Masterly and exquisite. . . . I quite squealed through it") tells a story of H'ry's having once wintered in Venice with a group of twenty friends whose primary occupation was "infinite talk, talk mainly, inexhaustibly, about persons and the 'personal equation' and the personal mystery." The Old World salon feel of the circle was challenged that season by the introduction of a young woman whose presence was welcomed both because she came well introduced and because they all knew that Old World salons had never made much room for "acclaimed and confident pretty girl[s]." The young woman acquitted herself admirably; the group took her into each of their "twenty social bosoms." It wasn't until H'ry returned from a short trip to Florence and Rome that he learned that the young woman's true purpose had been to amass a "treasure of impressions." She had published a letter in a "vulgar newspaper" revealing the group's "penetralia." She had been undercover! The gossiping crowd had itself become the subject of gossip! H'ry put the anecdote to use in *The Reverberator*'s tale of a marriage nearly derailed by carelessly slipped, and unscrupulously repeated, personal information.

It's difficult to imagine anyone more unsettled by gossip than H'ry. Whether it was over his bowels, his finances, or his love life (or lack of one), H'ry forever pleaded with W$^{\underline{m}}$ to not share information. Yet the letters—full of itineraries and rumors, caricatures and rants—reveal both W$^{\underline{m}}$ and H'ry as shameless gossipers themselves.

W$^{\underline{m}}$, in 1869: "That's all the gossip I can think of."

W$^{\underline{m}}$, in 1872: "I take up my long unwonted pen to make you a report of progress at home ensheathed in other gossip."

H'ry, in 1869: "Do in writing give more details gossip &c."

H'ry, in 1877: "Behold all the base gossip I can invent."

H'ry, in 1910, in the very last line of the very last letter of the correspondence, apologizing for his *need* to gossip: "Doing these things helps me, I find, most blessedly on."

H'ry took his lead on gossip from George Sand. In 1877, he recalled the preface to "André" in which Sand revealed that she had eavesdropped on her servants during a stay in Venice, ostensibly to acquaint herself with the local dialect, but in doing so coming into possession "of a large amount of local gossip." What this revealed to Sand was that men and women from all places tended to concern themselves with the same kinds of things. H'ry absorbed the motto: we were all alike in gossip.

And what do people tend to gossip about? We gossip over suggested facts of lives, over assertions that, correct or not, *seem* truer than what people will publicly attest to. Gossip is the excitement of ambiguity, of incomplete knowledge, of the tension between what you've heard and what you know. Drama results when the two don't jibe. We are alternately thrilled and terrified that the truth may out. The reading of others' letters stems from the same basic impulse: in letters, we are more honest than when we craft an argument or tell a story addressed to a broader audience. Literature rides the horse; letters peer into its mouth. H'ry believed this. A great deal of his early critical work is dedicated to the collected correspondence of other writers—Flaubert, Eliot, Balzac, St. Beuve, Lowell, Arnold, this a list of only the pieces that merited discussion in W^m and H'ry's own private exchange. (W^m's recommendation to H'ry of Goethe and Schiller's correspondence accidentally anticipates the effect of the brothers' letters: "The spectacle of two such earnestly living & working men is refreshing to the soul of any one, but in their aesthetic discussions you will find a particular profit I fancy.") Letters play an important role in H'ry's fiction as well. The tension is almost always the same: a letter has been written, what does the letter writer truly think, and who might come to know its contents? Again and again, characters confront the overwhelming impulse to interrupt the social contract and snatch up the delectable missive sitting in the crystal tray on the sideboard. There is no greater betrayal or drama than a stolen letter.

H'ry learned the hard way that a diary can be just as dramatic.

The problem with W^m and H'ry's "bottled-lightning" sister, Alice, seems to have been an inability to unstopper herself. Alice had the same mind as her favored brothers, and the great biographical question of her life is whether her intellectual talents went overlooked in the James family dynamic because she was sickly, or if she fell sick because her talents went overlooked. Alice started out life closer to her elder brother, but gravitated toward H'ry after W^m married. She followed H'ry to London, where he cared for her until she died of breast cancer in 1892. Though, like Proust, Alice is famous for having rarely left her bed, an active life in London came to her. She could go weeks without seeing H'ry, and her "Boston marriage" to Katherine Loring—like the lure of H'ry's sexuality—has cracked the wax seal of so many critical inkwells that one wishes that if Alice had been too-little unstoppered then critics might have remained more so. In any event, her own modest trickle of ink was how Alice ensured that even if she went overlooked she would not be forgotten. For the last several years of her life, she kept a copious diary, a soaring account of her mind and her suffering that included a range of juicy tidbits about those in the London social circle—gossip. Two years after she died, Katherine Loring had the manuscript typeset and bound in a tiny, four-copy edition.

"Oh yes, *please* send it to him!" H'ry said, when he first learned of the diary's existence. Katherine Loring had written to ask whether a copy could be forwarded to unfavored brother Bob. H'ry hadn't yet read the diary, and he regretted having given his assent as soon as he got his hands on it; it was filled, he told W$^{\underline{m}}$, with everything he had "gossiped to the sister." H'ry *liked* the diary—it was "heroic in its individuality, its independence"—and he was grateful to have it, as he had never had many letters from Alice. But he worried because in relating details that he now saw repeated, he was forced to admit that he had, on occasion, "'coloured' [things] to divert Alice!" He didn't know what Bob intended to do with the book. "I am troubled about it in every way," he wrote. What he hoped, he said, was that they could edit the diary ever so slightly "& then carefully burn with fire" the four extant copies. (H'ry failed in this, but the diary was not printed again in full until 1964.)

W$^{\underline{m}}$ thought H'ry was overreacting. "I don't see the *slightest* danger of any extracts from it floating about."

W^m had a wholly different attitude toward gossip. By the mid-1890s, he was active in the Society for Psychical Research—the investigation of supernatural phenomena—and on this front gossip was both a danger and a boon: on the one hand, gossip could explain how a false medium, intentionally or unwittingly, could give the impression of having come into possession of private knowledge; on the other, gossip was a tool that could and should be used, W^m suggested, to expand the reach of psychical research. Either way, he was far more dispassionate on the subject, which helps to explain why he often thought the "matter" of H'ry's fiction "too slight." Exactly those same societal pressures from which W^m seemed insulated—propriety, social status, reputation—shined bright in the backgrounds of H'ry's stories. In 1879, H'ry admitted that he was perplexed as to why W^m had remained cold to a particular tale. "I have got (heaven knows!) plenty of gravity within me," he wrote, "& I don't know why I can't put it more into the things I write."

On occasion, however, the concern ran the other way—and emotions flared. In January 1885, *The Bostonians* stirred anger among W^m's neighbors. A character in the story, "Miss Birdseye," seemed to local readers too close an analog to a certain "Miss Peabody," whom everyone knew to resemble the character and who even had the same identifying habit of misplacing her eyeglasses. W$\underline{m}$ hadn't yet read the book when he first complained that the furor was "a really pretty bad business." H'ry fumed at this. He'd meant no such association at all. He had known, of course, that titling the book *The Bostonians* would cause him to be "much abused," but the thing that really seemed to hurt was W$\underline{m}$'s thoughtlessness on the matter. "I have done nothing to deserve it," H'ry wrote, "& think your tone on the subject singularly harsh & unfair." Of course, a vague resemblance between Miss Birdseye and Miss Peabody had occurred to him as he wrote—but there had been no *intentional* attempt to render her. (The editors of the James correspondence note that "bird's eye" and "pea-body" mean the same thing.) And even if there had been, the image portrayed was "tenderly & sympathetically expressed." Indeed, the story would last "longer than poor Miss P.'s name or fame," and if anything she should have been grateful for the allusion. But the real problem was W$\underline{m}$. "The story is, I think, the best fiction I have written," H'ry wrote, "& I expected you, if you said any thing about it, would intimate that you thought as much—so that I find this charge on the subject of Miss P. a very cold douche indeed."

It took H'ry's angry letter nearly six weeks to arrive. W$^{\underline{m}}$ replied only briefly: "I trust your troubled soul is at rest." *The Bostonians* is the only major novel H'ry left out of the New York edition.

·14·

A decade later, as renowned as he would ever become but still smarting from the theater, H'ry began to feel the pressures of a too-active social life. Fame and family had produced a near endless string of visitors and dining obligations. His work was suffering as a result. In early February 1896, he attended a meeting of the Society for Psychical Research—an address of W$^{\underline{m}}$'s was presented by the organization's champion, Frederic Myers. "It had great success," H'ry wrote of the reading of W$^{\underline{m}}$'s address. "How worked & strained & overladen you must feel & how pitiful must seem to you my slow, small dribble of production."

H'ry was accompanied that evening by an unusual guest. Mrs. Mahlon Sands was a figure as tragic and prodigious as any of the women in H'ry's fiction. A transport from Newport, Rhode Island, Mrs. Sands and her husband had years earlier eased their way into the Marlborough House set, where she had become renowned for her beauty and wit ("The loveliest American that has yet dawned upon the world of London," claims a diplomat's memoir). She remained a fixture in society even after her husband died in a riding accident in 1888. It's not clear how she first met H'ry, but they seem to have formed something of a bond over the vexation of social obligation. In 1894, H'ry advised Mrs. Sands as to how she should approach sitting for John Singer Sargent. "You can't collaborate or co-operate, except by sitting still and looking beautiful," H'ry wrote. "Cultivate indifference, cultivate not looking at it or thinking about it." At Christmas, 1895, Mrs. Sands gifted H'ry a canary, a charming animal whose quiet comfort H'ry described to W^m after a season of endless visitors.

Mrs. Sands was a "great Psychist & devotee of yours," H'ry wrote in the same letter in which he reported on W^m's speech. He described Mrs. Sands in terms that reflected the tolls levied by social pressures: "She was a pathetic, *ballottée* creature—with nothing small or mean & with a beauty that had once been the greatest."

W^m sent Mrs. Sands a copy of his essay "Is Life Worth Living?," which was published as a small book in 1896. The essay would have affirmed Mrs. Sands's spiritualist interest. "Is Life Worth Living?" articulated the "will to believe" doctrine W^m had been working out through the 1880s and early 1890s, and amounted to a critical step on the path to pragmatism: we each have the right to supplement observable reality with an unseen spiritual order if only to thereby make life seem worth living. It's often argued that W^m was reflecting on his dark mood here, now a quarter-century past, but he was hardly alone: "That life is *not* worth living the whole army of suicides declare. . . . As we sit here in our comfort, [we] must 'ponder these things' also, for we are of one substance with these suicides, and their life is the life we share." W^m quoted Ruskin to contrast "the lightness of heart of a London dinner party" with those outside its walls, and then he tightened his focus onto what for Mrs. Sands must have seemed a familiar ennui: "My task, let me say now, is practically narrow, and my words are to deal only with that metaphysical *tedium vitæ* which is peculiar to reflecting men."

On July 24, 1896, H'ry passed along Mrs. Sands's gratitude for W^m's little book. Her note, H'ry said, arrived just at the climax of the London rush. He later recalled that she had implored him to visit her. "Are you not coming up at all?" she pleaded. "I am sick of the whole thing." Mrs. Sands died three days later. Her maid left the room for just a moment while dressing her for a dinner party. She had collapsed to the floor. "She had a weakness of heart," H'ry wrote. "That's all that's known."

Mrs. Sands was forty-one years old.

The death of Mrs. Sands illustrates what H'ry never stated: even if the "matter" of his fiction was light, the minds behind it lived and died as though it was very heavy indeed. He seemed to best understand this himself only after W^m fully fleshed out his system. "I can't now explain save by the very fact of the spell itself . . . that [*Pragmatism*] cast upon me," H'ry wrote in 1907. "All my life I have . . . unconsciously pragmatised." And in 1909, "As an artist & a 'creator' I can catch on, hold on, to pragmatism, & can work in the light of it & apply it." H'ry's fiction demonstrated W^m's "method of truth."

W^m was never able to be quite so gracious in return. Tempered by occasional praise, his criticisms of his brother's work started early, and never truly abated. In 1868, he lashed out at the "every day" elements of two of H'ry's early stories, and then explained his purpose: "I have uttered this long rigmarole in a dogmatic manner, as one speaks, to himself, but of course you will use it merely as a mass to react against in your own way, so that it may serve you some good purpose." He believed he was doing H'ry a service as he criticized a growing tendency toward "over-refinement" or "*curliness*" of style. "I think it ought to be of use to you," he wrote in 1872, "to have any detailed criticism fm even a wrong judge, and you don't get much fm. any one else." For the most part, H'ry agreed. "I hope you will continue to give me, when you can, your free impression of my performance. It is a great thing to have some one write to one of one's things as if one were a 3^d person & you are the only individual who will do this."

H'ry did not agree with all of W^m's "strictures." Some were clearly born of an overprotective spirit. Whenever W^m advised that H'ry bend toward the "newspaporial," or concentrate on writing of a "popular kind," H'ry kicked back. "The multitude, I am more & more convinced, have absolutely no taste—none at least that a thinking man is bound to defer to. To write for the few who have is doubtless to lose money—but I am not afraid of starving."

Long after H'ry had established a successful career, W^m worried that he would have to care for his brother in his old age. H'ry's bravado, however, and what he produced did not always jibe. He *was* afraid of starving. Even apart from his speculative sortie into the theater, his stories are often repetitive—he mined themes again and again, reselling the same idea to a range of venues—and he was well aware that some of his work was inferior. Ironically, this was the work that tended to please W^m most. When W^m praised "Longstaff's Marriage" and wondered why H'ry had left it out of a collection, H'ry dismissed the story as a "poor affair." And just a few months after the death of Mrs. Sands he disavowed an entire novel, *The Other House*, that W^m had enjoyed. "If *that's* what the idiots want," H'ry wrote, "I can give them their bellyfull."

W^m only grudgingly accepted H'ry's most ambitious methods. "It is superlatively well done," he wrote of *The Bostonians*, when he finally read it, "provided one admit that method of doing such a thing at all." The earnest criticism of the early letters gave way to banter as W^m struggled to comprehend whatever it was H'ry was trying to achieve. In 1905, flustered by *The Golden Bowl*, W^m called for something wholly new:

> But why won't you, just to please Brother, sit down and write a new book, with no twilight or mustiness in the plot, with great vigor and decisiveness in the action, no fencing in the

dialogue, no psychological commentaries, and
absolute straightness in the style?

H'ry replied with a wry broadside:

> I mean . . . to try to produce some uncanny
> form of thing, in fiction, that will gratify you,
> as Brother—but let me say, dear William, that
> I shall greatly be humiliated if you *do* like it, &
> thereby lump it, in your affection, with things,
> of the current age, that I have heard you express
> admiration for & that I would sooner descend
> to a dishonoured grave than have written.

More often, however, H'ry remained silent in response to W^m's frustration as they grew older. What
bothered W^m most was that now *everything* in H'ry's
fiction remained ambiguous. He couldn't imagine why
anyone would want to write in such a way ("[it] goes
agin the grain of all my own impulses in writing"), and
he couldn't leave it alone either. In 1907, he was still
trying to understand the difference in their methods:

> Mine being to say a thing in one sentence as
> straight and explicit as it can be made, and then

to drop it forever; yours being to avoid naming it straight, but by dint of breathing and sighing all round and round it, to arouse in the reader who may have had a similar perception already . . . the illusion of a solid object.

H'ry would never confirm whether W^m was on the right track in coming to understand his work, but he expressed disappointment that their mutual influence did not result in mutual appreciation:

I'm always sorry when I hear of your reading anything of mine, & always hope you won't—you seem to me so constitutionally unable to "enjoy" it, & so condemned to look at it from a point of view remotely alien to mine in writing it. . . . It shows how far apart & to what different ends we have had to work out . . . our respective intellectual lives. And yet I can read *you* with rapture.

H'ry must have been even more resigned than he was willing to admit. Was it not W^m who had once said that only works of imagination could lay effective siege to the philosophical battlements most worth attacking? Why did W^m fail to recognize that H'ry had volunteered for his army, and that in the war W^{m} waged H'ry was his fiercest champion and most decorated soldier?

·16·

On August 8, 1900, W^{m} related an embarrassing story. Throughout the summer, while traveling through Europe with his wife—named Alice, like the sister—he suffered from a range of symptoms: nervousness, heart trouble. He needed help, but didn't know where to turn. As it happened, he'd been receiving letters praising the work of a magnetic healer, a "Mrs. Melton" of Paris. W^{m} scoffed at Mrs. Melton, which had led to terrible fights with Alice. Even though W^{m} had long acted as a spiritualist leader, it was Alice who was more deeply beguiled by occult fads. Over the next few weeks, a variety of factors conspired to make Paris attractive: W^{m} got it in mind to seek an appointment with the city's great heart man, Pierre Potain, and an invitation to stay in a private Parisian home offered relief from an endless string of hotels. Perhaps most important, W^{m} told H'ry, a visit to the magnetic healer would convince Alice that "the powers of the occult world were not being neglected."

It was a mistake. Rather than relieving him of his ailments, the "nasty job" of Mrs. Melton's treatment succeeded only in producing boils. "I made an ass of myself letting that spider of hell the 'healer' touch me," W^{m} wrote.

His next few letters express the usual pleasure the brothers took in relating the history of awkward ailments. "The chief remaining furuncle broke this A.M." "The last boil is now disgorging its venomous heart." The peculiar fun of boil-breaking is corroborated by an account of Swami Vivekananda, who hosted a conclave of healers and modern mystics while W^{m} was in Paris. Vivekananda was honored by W^{m}'s attendance at the meeting, but he noted that the celebrated philosopher seemed distracted by careful self-ministrations from the opening gavel. W^{m}'s only memorable contribution to the proceedings came when one of the attendees proposed proving the existence of the "Fire God" by lighting a blaze in the parlor: W^{m} lifted his head from his pustule-worrying and announced that he might well have had something to say upon the Fire God if only he were not entirely occupied with the evolution of Meltonian blisters.

W^{m}'s attitude toward the magnetic healer challenges a long-standing scholarly assumption that his interest in psychical research depended on a suspension of a critical faculty that would have better off left intact. Like the sciences whose methodology they imitate, history and biography crave contrast and absolutes and are therefore ill-prepared to survey enthusiasm tempered by skepticism. W$^{\underline{m}}$ was a believer (To H'ry, 1906: "There is *something* back there that shows that minds communicate, even those of the dead with those of the living"), but he was also a scientist who knew that he'd never proven a damn thing when it came to ghosts, prayer, or magical healing. That hardly mattered. His entire career was an attempt to form a practical response, rooted in the measurable and observable, to the fact that reality was ambiguous and appeared intent on staying that way. The study of séances and spirits might never yield proof of anything, yet it had the value of exploration: "occult" was a name for that which accepted psychological knowledge could only glimpse in the shadows of the not yet known and perhaps immeasurable. H'ry's reaction to all this was equally complicated. As the years had passed, he had grown quite close to W$^{\underline{m}}$'s wife, Alice (they would live together, after W$^{\underline{m}}$ died), and her letters to him speak of her "sittings" as though he is a confederate in belief. On at least one occasion H'ry asked that W^m phone a medium to arrange a series of séances for him. Yet even more than W^m, H'ry seemed to recognize that W^m's interest in the occult was an attempt to combine his psychology with his philosophy, his willingness to believe with his sickly soulfulness, and that all of it was an expression of a society so bored and weary of itself that it was actually ill and needed to be reminded that life was worth living.

·17·

In August 1889—a dozen years before the plague of Meltonian blisters—W^m returned to Boston after a long, lone trip to Europe. It was just at that moment when his life had begun to settle in. *The Principles of Psychology* was almost complete, and teaching offered financial security and a comfortable routine. Alice and the children were staying at the summerhouse in New Hampshire he'd bought not long before, and W^m himself was lodging with friends in Cambridge while builders completed a new family home on Irving Street. He could see the almost-finished house from his temporary bedroom window. Early one morning, still in his nightshirt, he rose and peered out at a dim, uncanny world. Past and future seemed to collide: the little town accounted for the majority of his history, and he would live there for the rest of his life. He wrote to his brother of the peculiar feeling of the moment. The letter is lost, but H'ry took careful note of it: "Gazing at your house in the August dawn—it must have seemed queer indeed, with all the dead past putting in such an appearance at the same time."

A return from Europe, a suspension between past and future, and queer sensations experienced at odd hours are all elements of "The Jolly Corner," one of H'ry's most famous ghost stories, published in 1907.

Ghosts, for H'ry—Virginia Woolf claimed several years after he died that his handful of ghost stories were the best of his work—spoke far less to what might be true of the natural world than to memory and the past. In 1899, when W$^{\underline{m}}$ sent him a short note preserved from Henry Sr.'s youth, H'ry offered thanks for the "beautiful, innocent ghostly [letter] from Father's 19th year." Ghosts were a much-trodden route to psychological projection even before H'ry's preface to "Sir Edmund Orme" (W$^{\underline{m}}$: "Perfect [thing] . . . which I enjoyed *extremely*") claimed that "hauntedness" was romantic parlance for "unconscious obsession." H'ry could be either lighthearted about psychical research, as when he called on W^m to exert psychical pressure to ensure his success in the theater—"This is really the time to show your stuff"—or quietly critical, as in "Maud Evelyn," a story in which a psychically inclined couple arrange a suitor for their dead daughter: the couple is portrayed as foolishly aggrieved, but their willingness to believe leads them to pragmatic contentedness, so who could argue with them? (W^m, apparently: when Alice read it aloud to him, he judged it "very exquisite but hardly realistic.") H'ry's real problem with psychical research was that, as ghost stories went, the scientific study of psychical phenomena didn't yield particularly effective tales. In his preface to *The Turn of the Screw*, he argued that "correct" ghosts—ghosts that adhered to the kind of blasé, inexpressive incident clogging the psychical record—would make but "poor subjects" in stories that must absolutely aspire to action and drama. Indeed, the apparitions of *The Turn of the Screw*, Peter Quint and Miss Jessel, were "not 'ghosts' at all" in the traditional sense. Rather, they worked by helping H'ry express his "subject all directly and intensely." In other words, his ghosts were like his girls: they were symbols, figures, figments of the humanity that they spookily and portentously reflected.

All this seems to have been lost on W^m, who, like those female readers prone to projecting themselves onto Daisy Miller or Milly Theale, was apt to thinking of literal inspiration. Throughout the letters W^m attempts to feed H'ry names and plots. He believed he recognized himself in *The American*'s "morbid little clergyman," and he once offered up his wife as a possible character. No experience W^m ever had, however, was richer in potential material, he thought, than a particular night involving his psychical confrere Frederic Myers.

About six months before W^m subjected himself to magnetic tortures, he and Alice stayed for a time in Carqueiranne, a resort town on the southern tip of France. They were accompanied by Myers; his wife, Silvia; and a "Mrs. Thompson," a medium whom Myers held forth as proof of a world beyond the knowable universe. Myers's relationship with Mrs. Thompson was mysterious, even to his wife, and late one night the heated threesome burst in on W^m and Alice's late-burning fire. Could they arbitrate a dispute? W^m and

Alice cowrote an account of the incident for H'ry—the ensuing scene was ripe with lies, suggestions, and adumbrations—and the great tragedy of it, once everyone had returned to their rooms, was that H'ry had not been there to be impressed by it. It was just up H'ry's line of "grotesque humors," W^{m} fretted, strutting up and down the room, both for its three main players, and for Frederic and Silvia Myers's two young children. "A queer pair," W^{m} noted, "reminding me irresistibly of the two in the turn of the screw."

H'ry was interested in the story for its gossip value— "You must give me details when we meet—they will be very interesting"—but did he think the scene might make for a good tale? Probably not. H'ry would have disagreed with Woolf that his ghost stories were his best work (he derided even *The Turn of the Screw* as a "potboiler"), and the moments from W^{m}'s letters that inspired him most were not the suggestions of drama-laden plots, but the quiet intervals that W^{m} sometimes took care to describe, moments full of atmosphere and details that communicated mood and sensibility. As well, H'ry's imagination by then must have already been burbling on *The Wings of the Dove*, even though he wouldn't sign a contract for the book for another few months. Written notably in the same time period when W^m was completing *The Varieties of Religious Experience*, *The Wings of the Dove* combines H'ry's most ambitious impulses as a writer with an attempt to take on a story with a matter large enough for W^m's taste. He completed it in the light of one final glimpse into the rift that separated him from his brother.

·18·

In Carqueiranne, at a quieter moment, W^m and Frederic Myers sat together with Mrs. Thompson and asked her what the future held. She predicted that W^m would soon recover from his various illnesses, and that Myers would be dead within two years. The men laughed, as the reverse seemed much more likely. Mrs. Thompson was wrong, but only in that her view of Myers's demise was shortsighted. He was dead in ten months.

On January 17, 1901, W^m dictated a letter describing Myers's death vigil in Rome. Myers had been struck by double pneumonia, and W^m had prescribed morphia when it became clear how far the disease had advanced. The death rattle had begun that morning. Myers had asked to be read to, and was read to. Now, it was 8:45

P.M. and W^m sat before an open stove, speaking aloud a letter to H'ry, which Alice recorded under the light of an electric table-lamp. Myers died forty-five minutes later.

For W^m, the scene was particularly painful because Myers was a symbol of why the work of the Society for Psychical Research was important. "The official psychologists affect to look down on him," W^m wrote, "but he has perhaps done more for psychology than any of the lot." This was even truer of W^m than it was of Myers.

What's notable about the scene now is what they chose to read to Myers on his deathbed. Both Alice and W^m were particularly fond of H'ry's early travel sketches, and W^m in particular liked to have certain descriptive passages read to him before he went to sleep. Alice would read a paragraph, and W^m would say, "Read it again." When Myers asked to be read to, H'ry's *Transatlantic Sketches*, published twenty-five years earlier, was close at hand. The letters specify that Myers responded thoughtfully to "Roman Neighborhoods," which features "the picturesque amid picturesqueness," a description of Lake Albano, a few miles southeast of Rome:

105

This beautiful pool—it is hardly more—occupies
the crater of a prehistoric volcano—a perfect
cup, moulded and smelted by furnace-fires. The
rim of the cup rises high and densely wooded
around the placid, stone-blue water, with a sort
of natural artificiality. The sweep and contour of
the long circle are admirable; never was a lake so
charmingly lodged. It is said to be of extraordinary
depth; and though stone-blue water seems at
first a very innocent substitute for boiling lava,
it has a sinister look which betrays its dangerous
antecedents. The winds never reach it, and its
surface is never ruffled; but its deep-bosomed
placidity seems to cover guilty secrets, and you
fancy it in communication with the capricious
and treacherous forces of nature. Its very color
has a kind of joyless beauty—a blue as cold and
opaque as a solidified sheet of lava. Streaked and
wrinkled by a mysterious motion of its own, it
seemed the very type of a legendary pool, and
I could easily have believed that I had only to sit
long enough into the evening to see the ghosts of
classic nymphs and naiads cleave its sullen flood
and beckon to me with irresistible arms.

If H'ry ever replied to "Roman Neighborhoods" being read at Myers's deathbed, the letter is lost. But it would not have been lost on him that the scene demonstrated that everything he'd written in a quarter-century of letters about his growing distaste for the picturesque had gone ignored. The very same letter that described Myers's final expiration noted that W$^{\underline{m}}$ and Alice had that same evening read H'ry's essay on Thackeray and Rye—the piece in which he had dismissed the usefulness of description. W$^{\underline{m}}$ claimed they had read the essay "with much pleasure," but the truth was that the point of it had been either missed or dismissed.

H'ry drew a distinction between a popular audience's reaction to art and the reaction one received from a "finer interest"—a coy way, really, of referring to his own interest in literature, and to the interest he hoped to inspire in others. What he meant was technique, a reader not *passively* reading a story, but coming to recognize that part of the intended pleasure of some books was the reader becoming keenly aware of the conscription of his or her intellect into the service of the story's process. All stories relied on readers' imaginations, surely, but the stories that were most worthwhile were the ones that set out to satisfy the finer interest's craving for *how* the story produced its satisfaction. H'ry's own finer interest in his description of Lake Albano—one W^m certainly should have sensed—would have been that it was a metaphorically fluid treatment of a literally fluid subject: his brother's stream of consciousness applied to a body of water. Rather than taking a variety of angles on a particular object in a futile attempt to render it factually, the description started with the impression of the lake, an impression that triggered a stream of additional impressions, and that plurality of impressions made it a portrait not of the lake, but of the mind that was perceiving it, which was the more important subject anyway.

And that's a fair description of the inner workings of *The Wings of the Dove*, composed almost entirely of streaming minds depicted in the process of anticipating events, and then—after a jump—reflecting on those same events having already happened. Actual events are snipped away as neatly as "gig" from "whirligig." The theater lights on the foreground action have dimmed, and a bright spotlight searches and darts among the shadows of consciousness in the background.

But what of the larger matter that W^m had called for, and had kept on calling for? As early as 1879, reacting to W^m's pleas for a real story, H'ry admitted to being intimidated by overly dramatic plots:

> It comes from modesty & delicacy . . . or at least from the high state of development of my artistic conscience, which is so greatly attached to *form* that it shrinks from believing that it can supply it properly for *big* subjects, & yet it is constantly studying the way to do so; so that at least, I am sure, it will arrive.

He seems to have been thinking of this exchange thirty years later when he began his preface to *The Wings of the Dove* with the claim that the story stemmed from a "very old—if I shouldn't perhaps say a very young—motive." He worried that the story of a dying girl would seem like a shortcut to drama, but he reminded his readers that Milly Theale's tragic state was "but half the case, the correlative half being the state of others as affected by her." How exactly this worked was the entire point, and he advised his readers to take careful note of his "positively close and felicitous application of method." What method? Even in the preface this is described with extended water metaphors. Characters' consciousnesses will be "decanted" for us. We will find ourselves "saturated" with sensibilities. The plot "comes to a head." Compared to a simple travelogue, this particular experience of Venice is a "deeper draught out of a larger cup." Milly Theale's terminal fate creates all around her "very much that whirlpool of movement of the waters produced by the sinking of a big vessel."

The book takes it even further. A profession of love is likened to "a tide breaking through," and language itself feels like "plashes of a slow, thick tide." Imagination has a "high-water" mark, and confusion feels like butting up "against a firm object in the stream." A desire to confess is likened to an impulse to "overflow" from a "deeper reserve," and even Merton Densher muses that a moment of anxiety would be best "likened to the rapids of Niagara." It's Densher, too, who recognizes that each of the characters' various streams of thought stem from a single source and flow toward a common reservoir:

> All of which . . . sharpened his sense of
> immersion in an element more strangely than
> agreeably warm—a sense that was moreover,

during the next two or three hours, to be fed
to satiety by several other impressions. . . .
There was a deeper depth of it, doubtless, for
some than for others; what he, at any rate, in
particular knew of it was that he seemed to
stand in it up to his neck. He moved about in it,
and it made no plash; he floated, he noiselessly
swam in it; and they were all together, for that
matter, like fishes in a crystal pool.

W^m recognized none of this when he read *The Wings
of the Dove*. He was left befuddled, crying out over
why H'ry would want to tell stories that told, actually, nothing. "My stuff, such as it is," H'ry replied, "is
inevitable—for *me*." A few months later, a short time
before W^m left for a scheduled meeting with unfavored
brother Bob, H'ry gave W^m a hint veiled as a goodwill
wish:

May you be floated grandly over your cataract—
by which I don't mean have any manner of *fall*,
but only be a Niagara of eloquence, all continuously, whether above or below the rapids.

W^m may have preferred that H'ry write only of the literal, but that didn't mean he was incapable of metaphoric or figurative language himself, particularly when it came to water imagery. In 1899, reacting to the warmongering of Governor Teddy Roosevelt, W^m leveled a charge of abstractness in the *Boston Evening Transcript.* "[Roosevelt] gushes over war as the ideal condition of human society," W^m wrote. "He swamps everything together in one flood of abstract bellicose emotion."

If H'ry thought that the charge of abstractness might apply to him as well, he buried it beneath a general malaise. "You have an admirable eloquence," he wrote of W^m's argument. "But the age is *all* to the vulgar."

By the late 1890s, W^m was a well-known public intellectual. He had begun lending his name to campaigns against wrongs ranging from vivisection, which he had promoted as a younger man, to an imperialist spirit grown rampant in the country. He may have felt even more responsible for the latter. In "Is Life Worth Living?" and "What Makes a Life Significant?" he had argued that cultivating a certain "strenuousness" gave life its finest interest. This had been warped into Roosevelt's "The Strenuous Life" (Roosevelt had been W$^{\underline{m}}$'s student at Harvard), which employed a latent militant spirit as a fulcrum for utopian idealism. W$^{\underline{m}}$ tried to countermand this in *The Varieties of Religious Experience*, which argued that the "real strenuous life" was the one that was lived *as if* God existed—that is, a life in which decisions and actions were made to chime with a good one could sense afoot in the universe. *The Varieties of Religious Experience* was a wild success, but it did nothing to prevent the country's descent into imperial aggression, and soon the United States was occupying the Philippines, where in W$^{\underline{m}}$'s view his country was merely acting as pirate. H'ry agreed. The only thing that had so far offered balance to his country's "crudities" was the fact that until then it had no record of overseas murder and theft. *"Terminato—terminato!"* he wrote W$^{\underline{m}}$. "One would like to be a Swiss or a Montenegrian now."

In the years following *The Varieties of Religious Experience* and *The Wings of the Dove*, W$^{\underline{m}}$ and H'ry remained productive, but the rest of the decade proved disappointing for both of them. In 1907, W$^{\underline{m}}$ told H'ry that

113

he wouldn't be surprised if *Pragmatism* triggered in philosophy something like "the protestant reformation." It didn't, and soon enough he was handing off the reins of even psychology to Sigmund Freud. That same year, publication began of the twenty-four volumes of H'ry's New York edition, each furnished with a 7,000-word preface. H'ry hoped for remuneration, but the books sold poorly.

If the brothers had gestated together in the womb of art, then their crib was a utopian spirit heady in the 1840s, the time of their extreme youth. Henry Sr. was an ardent follower of Emanuel Swedenborg and Charles Fourier, and at least one biographer has likened the James family household to a "stale phalanstery," after Fourier's vision of the perfect living arrangement. Utopian imagery recurs throughout the letters. A note from W^m during his time in Brazil is addressed from the "Original Seat of Garden of Eden," and in 1877 H'ry anticipated that his letter to W^m in Newport would find him "wrapped up in the enchantments of Paradise"—that is, reclining under a cedar in the same landscape John La Farge had painted.

Utopian enthusiasm faded in the 1850s with the failure of the social experiments of Fourier and Robert

Owen, but it surged again in the 1890s in the wake of successful, idealistic novels by Samuel Butler, William Morris, Edward Bellamy, and many others. W$^{\underline{m}}$ must have felt pounded by opposing tides. On the one hand, his argument for a strenuous life had backfired horrifically, and on the other, he had always been suspicious of schemes based on too-generous assessments of human nature. He had once written that the instinct toward ownership "discredit[ed] in advance all radical forms of communistic utopia," and, even if it hadn't, could the race truly be said to have outgrown the bloodlust that penetrated every nook of history? "The old human instincts of war-making and conquest," W$^{\underline{m}}$ wrote H'ry in 1899, "sweep all principles away before them." Still, W$^{\underline{m}}$ had tried. In an age of failed systems, he had proposed a system of his own, pragmatism, rooted in history and designed to avoid the hubris that doomed its predecessors. But it failed, too. Wholly committed to measuring the value of ideas with observable results, W$^{\underline{m}}$ must have wondered what it was that his own work bequeathed.

H'ry made himself useful in this regard. He had watched and read as W$^{\underline{m}}$ had waged a campaign against utopian visions, lashing out at stale philosophies and highly regarded communities like Chautauqua, New York. Just as he had gently nudged W^m along during his development as a psychologist, H'ry now made quiet overtures on behalf of a better world. In 1905, he made particular note of an essay of W^m's celebrating a Scottish philosopher who had advocated a kind of communal living, and a few months later H'ry suggested that W^m read Wells's *A Modern Utopia* ("Remarkable for other things than for his characteristic cheek"). About a month after that W^m swooned over the beauty of Stanford, where he had arrived to teach a course: "It is utopian."

In the interim he'd produced one of his most famous essays, "The Moral Equivalent of War," which he delivered as a speech at Stanford on February 25, 1906. The essay weaves several concepts that W^m had tried out on H'ry over the years. "Our ancestors have bred pugnacity into our bone and marrow, and thousands of years of peace won't breed it out of us," he wrote, expanding on his Philippines letter from just a few years earlier. The essay's argument that calamity breeds community seems drawn from W^m's description to H'ry of the Boston fire of 1872: "Rich men suffered but upon the community at large I shd. say its effect had been rather exhilarating than otherwise." Finally, "The Moral Equivalent of War" taps into the letters' slow current of utopian preoccupation: its first utopian note characterizes an ongoing ideological battle in the public sphere—warhawks versus peaceniks—as "but one utopia against another." In reply, W$^{\underline{m}}$ confesses to his own "utopian hypothesis," an unlikely twining together of man's worst impulse with his best: the establishment of a "corps" of youth that would rally against natural disasters whenever and wherever they occurred. The benefits would be legion:

> The military ideals of hardihood and discipline would be wrought into the glowing fibre of the people; no one would remain blind as the luxurious classes now are blind, to man's real relations to the globe he lives on.

W$^{\underline{m}}$ didn't live to see it, but "The Moral Equivalent of War" laid the foundation for the most measurable and observable results of his work: the Civilian Conservation Corps, the Peace Corps, and Americorps.

He didn't have to wait long at all, however, for first-hand proof of his basic thesis. Six weeks later, at 5:30 on the morning of April 18, 1906, he and Alice were woken by the great San Francisco earthquake. W^m published an essay about the experience in *Youth's Companion*, though its rough draft was a letter he wrote to H'ry four days after the quake struck. The experience thrilled him, he wrote. When he first woke, he gleefully climbed to his hands and knees on the bed. The tremors—it would have been easy to mistake it for an ornery divinity—slowly *crescendoed* and then finally shook the room "like a rat by a terrier." When it was all over W^m accompanied a companion down into the city. The damage was dreadful, but what was most notable was the order that prevailed among the survivors. Even criminals, W^m claimed, had been solemnized and inspired to virtue by the occasion. "I would n't have missed this Stanford experience for anything," he wrote H'ry, "because it has been so *vivid*."

It was perhaps even more vivid for H'ry, who suffered terribly ("I am . . . as limp & spent as if I had been hanging 14 days by my heels") until word came that W^m and Alice were safe. Nervous as he was, though, it's hard to imagine he would have missed the irony. Not only had he coaxed a utopia out of W^m in the nick of time, he had done so at almost the same moment he proposed one of his own. Characteristically, W^m had offered an actual solution to an actual disaster. H'ry's was wholly figurative.

"The Question of Our Speech," which H'ry delivered on a number of occasions during his travels for *The American Scene*, painted a near-on apocalyptic view of the state of elocution. Language was itself a kind of Jamesian heroine, a "transported maiden," an "unrescued Andromeda," and the state we found ourselves in was one in which we were cut off from her, from "her taste and her genius." A world without correct speech was "evil," H'ry said, and "to accept that doom [was] simply to accept the doom of the slovenly." But all was not lost. Contact and communication could of course bring about the "happy state." We did not have to rely on inadequate instincts. Through an act of will we could train ourselves, acquire a "second nature," a more "acute consciousness." The better world was not lost:

> Keep up your hearts, all the same, keep them up to the pitch of confidence in that "second nature" of which I speak; the perfect possession of this highest of civilities, the sight, through the narrow portal, of the blue horizon across the valley, the wide fair country in which your effort will have

settled to the most exquisite of instincts, in which you will taste all the savor of the gathered fruit, and in which perhaps, at last, *then*, "in solemn troops and sweet societies," you may, sounding the clearer notes of intercourse as only women can, become yourselves models and missionaries, perhaps a little even martyrs, of the good cause.

·20·

In 1877, H'ry reviewed a newly published two-volume set of Balzac's letters. He was embarrassed by the books. Balzac was coarse, driven by egotism, ungraceful, and blind to all but his personal concerns and ambition. "The contents . . . are so private, so personal," H'ry wrote, "that the generous critic constantly lays them down with a sort of dismay, and asks himself in virtue of what particular privilege or what newly discovered principle it is, that he is thus burying his nose in them."

W^m had an answer. In "Is Life Worth Living?" he cited two good reasons for sick souls distracted by thoughts of the abyss to plod along for at least another twenty-four hours: the daily newspaper, and "to see . . . what the next postman will bring."

Letter writing could be a terrible burden, and both brothers buckled under the strain of it.

W^m, in 1883: "For three or 4 weeks in London I did *nothing* literally *nothing*, but write letters, day after day."

H'ry, in 1887: "I come back to life, as it were, to meet a mountain of letters, & I have lost a whole month of time."

Yet the only thing worse than their composition was the wait to receive a letter.

W^m, in 1869: "Verily, it is worthwhile pining for letters for 3 weeks to know the exquisite joy of relief."

H'ry, in 1873: "What a poor business is writing after all! Answer my letter nevertheless."

The very best of W^m and H'ry's letters contain neither news, nor gossip, nor arguments, nor drafts of philosophies. They are self-portraits:

H'ry, in 1870, from Great Malvern:

It's a horrible afternoon—a piercing blast, a driving snow storm & my spirits *à l'avenant*. I have had a cheery British fire made up in my dingy British bedroom & have thus sate me down to this ghastly mockery of a fraternal talk.

W^m, in 1872, from southern Maine:

I write in the little parlor opposite the Office—
4:30 P.M.—the steady heavy roaring of the surf
comes through the open window borne by
the delicious salt breeze over the great bank of
stooping willows, field and fence. The little horse
chestnuts are as big, the cow with the board face
still crops the grass. The broad sky & sea are
whanging with the mellow light. All is as it was
& will be.

Like perfumed paper shipped to a long-dead lover,
even a letter addressed to another puffs up a whiff of
human frailty and warmth.

NOTES

I, II, III: The Correspondence of William James: William and Henry,
   Vols. 1–3 (Charlottesville: University Press of Virginia,
   1992–1994).

Writings 1878–1899: Writings 1878–1899, William James (New York:
   Library of America, 1992).

Writings 1902–1910: Writings 1902–1910, William James (New York:
   Library of America, 1987).

The Question: The Question of Our Speech and The Lesson of Balzac,
   Henry James (Boston: Houghton, Mifflin, 1905).

Wings: The Wings of the Dove, Henry James (New York: Modern
   Library, 1937).

To Whom It May Concern

"to anyone . . ." *Journals and Miscellaneous Notebooks of Ralph
   Waldo Emerson*, ed. William H. Gilman (Cambridge, Mass.:
   Harvard University Press, 1960–1982), vol. 7, p. 405

·1·

"Mr. James . . ." *I*, p. 1 (corrected slightly for punctuation)
"Sweet was . . ." *I*, p. 1
"my little array . . ." *I*, p. 2
"Drear and . . ." *I*, p. 1
"I'd give my . . ." *I*, p. 91
"Among the letters . . ." *I*, p. 9

"What would n't . . ." *I*, p. 30

"I'd give . . ." *I*, p. 40

"I wish I . . ." *I*, p. 77

"heaviest days . . ." *I*, p. 82

"Oh call my brother . . ." *I*, p. 81 (the poem is Felicia Dorothea
  Hermans's "The Child's First Grief")

"my in many . . ." *I*, p. 193

"Your letter . . ." *I*, p. 270

"I would give . . ." *I*, p. 366

"Would to God . . ." *II*, p. 45

"I long to . . ." *II*, p. 111

"How I wish . . ." *II*, p. 416

"Within the last . . ." *III*, p. 66 (corrected slightly)

"formed part . . ." *II*, p. 290

"Where the river . . ." *The Poems of Matthew Arnold, 1840–1867*
  (London: Oxford University Press, 1909), p. 195

"And the width . . ." *II*, p. 290

"Oh for . . ." *III*, p. 411

"An immense . . ." *III*, p. 419

·2·

"I am more . . ." *I*, p. 13

"[It] would . . ." *II*, p. 37

"There is *no* . . ." *II*, p. 44

"tired as . . ." *III*, p. 154

"A stage . . ." *I*, p. 88

"damnable nausea . . ." *I*, pp. 285–286

"consequently . . ." *I*, p. 369

"you sweat . . ." *I*, p. 91

"my spirits . . ." *I*, p. 116

"Have just . . ." *II*, p. 21

"[This] is . . ." *II*, p 65

"the very blight . . ." *II*, p. 57

"Painful boils . . ." *I*, p. 78

"Christian . . ." *III*, p. 126

"fill a day . . ." *III*, p. 126

"It must seem . . ." *II*, p. 142

"in state of . . ." *II*, p. 407

"put inside . . ." *I*, p. 113

"I blush . . ." *I*, p. 84

"Never . . ." I, p. 78

"I may . . ." *I*, p. 105

"Sighs . . ." *I*, p. 158

"violent . . ." *I*, p. 108

"by the insertion . . ." *I*, p. 108

"These reflections . . ." *I*, p. 110 (slight editorial change omitted)

"moving . . ." *I*, p. 138

"But my diagnosis . . ." *III*, p. 410

·3·

"If you wish . . ." *I*, p. 272

"It is a . . ." *I*, p. 23

"the mask is . . ." *I*, p. 28

"in the head . . ." *The Principles of Psychology*, vol. 1, William
    James (London: Macmillan, 1891), p. 301

"I would give . . ." *I*, p. 74

"Mysterious & . . ." *I*, p. 206

"a procession . . ." *Writings 1878–1899*, p. 911

"Our mental life . . ." Ibid., p. 987

"fascinated by . . ." *II*, p. 133

"Our minds are . . ." "The Hidden Self," William James, *Scribner's Magazine*, no. 7 (March 1890), p. 364

"Most of it . . ." *II*, p. 150

"Consciousness, then . . ." *Writings 1878–1899*, p. 159

"debauch on . . ." *I*, p. 21

"French literature . . ." "The Hidden Self," William James, *Scribner's Magazine*, no. 7 (March 1890), p. 362

"The notion of . . ." *Writings 1902–1910*, p. 776

"blind to . . ." *Writings 1878–1899*, p. 841

"the true philosophy . . ." *II*, p. 373

"no man lives . . ." Stevenson's essay is quoted at length in "On a Certain Blindness in Human Beings," *Writings 1878–1899*, p. 847

"I believe . . ." *I*, p. 203

"There seems . . ." *I*, p. 210

"bloom with . . ." *I*, p. 313

"read it with . . ." *I*, p. 46

"the picture of . . ." *Complete Stories: 1864–1874*, Henry James (New York: Library of America, 1999), p. 769

"'étude' style . . ." *I*, p. 27

"to adumbrate by . . ." *Writings 1878–1899*, pp. 946–947

"the lively . . ." *The Turn of the Screw and Other Stories*, Henry James (Oxford: Oxford University Press, 1992), p. liii

"He was conscious . . ." *The Tragic Muse*, Henry James (New York: Penguin, 1995), p. 169

"I still think . . ." "A Case of Automatic Drawing," William James, *Popular Science Monthly*, no. 64 (January 1904), p. 200

"proceeds from . . ." *The Question*, p. 80

"I am reading . . ." *III*, p. 210

"the stiff breeze . . ." *The Question*, p. 61

"the pride . . . ," "hardly . . . curious . . ." Ibid., p. 60

"to say where . . ." Ibid., p. 93

"figures representing . . ." Ibid., p. 86

"greater quantity . . ." Ibid., p. 83

"from their point . . ." Ibid., p. 98

"the *image* . . ." Ibid., p. 71

"*how* we . . ." Ibid., p. 106

"into the . . ." Ibid., p. 98

"We thus walk . . ." Ibid., pp. 89–90

·4·

"the mysterious . . ." *Writings 1878–1899*, p. 846

"Your article . . ." *I*, p. 22

"dressed in cast . . ." *I*, p. 20

"It is . . ." "Historical Novels," Henry James, *Nation*, August 15, 1867, p. 126

"sweating fearfully . . ." *I*, p. 18

"[He has] an extreme . . ." *I*, p. 19

"outside of the . . . ," "I've no doubt . . . ," "the one . . . ," "mere fact . . ." *I*, p. 40

"higher and . . . ," "vague tirade . . ." *I*, p. 41

"the father . . ." *The Question*, p. 67

"blasted artistic . . ." *I*, p. 190

"a sort of . . ." *I*, p. 268

"a dead . . ." *I*, p. 271

"George Eliot is . . ." "*Daniel Deronda*: A Conversation," Henry James, *Atlantic Monthly* (December 1876), p. 687

"G.S. babbles . . ." *I*, p. 56

"it impossible . . ." *I*, p. 273

"Something even . . ." "George Sand," Henry James, *Galaxy*
    (July 1877), p. 64

"[I] think I may . . ." *I*, p. 46

·5·

"need not press . . ." *The Question*, p. 72

"It is again . . ." *II*, p. 278

"It's a strange . . ." *III*, p. 1

"dancing a . . ." *The Correspondence of William James*, ed. Ignas
    K. Sprupskelis and Elizabeth M. Berkeley, vol. 4 (Charlottes-
    ville: University Press of Virginia), p. 244

"the whirligig . . ." *Essays in Psychical Research*, William James
    (Cambridge, Mass.: Harvard University Press, 1986), p. 137

"The wheel of . . ." *III*, p. 300

"The term I . . ." *The American Scene*, Henry James (London:
    Chapman and Hall, 1907), p. 206

"If I were . . ." *Complete Stories: 1864–1874*, Henry James (New
    York: Library of America, 1999), pp. 272–273

"the story . . ." *II*, p. 143

"throws much . . ." *III*, p. 389

"approach her . . ." *Wings*, p. xxii

"She worked . . ." Ibid., p. 88

·6·

"spurn . . ." *I*, p. 67

"I feel as . . ." *I*, p. 68

"It was a . . ." *I*, p. 69

"I never . . ." *I*, p. 133

128

"Your eyes . . ." *The Jameses*, R. W. B. Lewis (New York: Farrar, Straus and Giroux, 1991), p. 109

"world of . . ." *The Three Jameses*, C. Harley Grattan (New York: New York University Press, 1962), p. 215

"All art is . . ." *The Tragic Muse*, Henry James (New York: Penguin, 1995), p. 23

"[Spencer] regards . . ." *Writings 1878–1899*, p. 929

"My experience . . ." Ibid., pp. 929–930

"Experience proceeds . . ." Ibid., p. 925

"has grown . . ." *II*, p. 47

"I doubt . . ." *I*, p. 206

"I sometimes . . ." *II*, p. 380

"It is impossible . . ." "Winchelsea, Rye, and *Denis Duval*," Henry James, *Scribner's Magazine* (January 1901), p. 47

"Most *perfect* . . ." *II*, p. 241

"His impression . . ." *The Turn of the Screw and The Lesson of the Master*, Henry James (New York: Modern Library, 1930), p. 192

"With . . . your tragic . . ." *II*, p. 146

"She only watched . . ." *The Tragic Muse*, Henry James (New York: Penguin, 1995), p. 303

"To day is a . . ." *I*, p. 231

"This strict fusion . . ." "The Novels of Mr. Henry James," Percy Lubbock, *Times Literary Supplement*, July 8, 1909

·7·

"What a *deprecatory* . . ." "What Is an Emotion?" William James, *Mind* (April 1884), p. 202

"I can't give . . ." *I*, p. 380

"his readers . . ." *The Academy: A Weekly Review of Literature, Science, and Art*, April 19, 1884, p. 278

"to give a . . ." *Writings 1878–1899*, p. 945

"But if you . . ." Ibid.

"I needn't dilate . . ." *I*, p. 121

"Alack! . . ." *I*, p. 134

"On the spot . . ." *I*, p. 133

"I can well . . ." *I*, p. 128

"lay the basis . . ." *I*, p. 76

"prompter . . ." *I*, p. 143

"irradiating . . ." *I*, p. 144

"He belongs . . . ," "strike[s] you . . ." *I*, p. 94

"I should be . . . ," "I'd give . . ." *I*, p. 95

"so far . . . ," "a great . . ." *I*, p. 134

"a Veronese picture . . ." *Wings*, p. 377

"almost as if . . ." Ibid., p. 169

·8·

"But I envy . . ." *I*, p. 165

"This chapter . . ." *Writings 1878–1899*, p. 153

"yet a painter . . ." Ibid., p. 155

"Very exquisitely . . ." *I*, p. 103

"What does the . . ." *Complete Stories*, p. 460

"as big as all . . . ," "He ought . . ." *I*, p. 101

·9·

"a class of . . . ," "There was nothing . . ." *The Human Comedy*, Honoré de Balzac (New York: Peter Fenelon Collier, 2008), p. 29

"5, or 6 . . ." *III*, p. 279

"common schools . . ." *The Question*, p. 44

"avoiding vulgarity . . . ," "the barking . . ." Ibid., p. 16

"pomposity . . ." *I*, p. 18

"[He] has a sense . . ." *I*, p. 262

"the determination . . ." *I*, p. 346

"a certain impression . . ." *I*, p. 36

"There wd. be . . ." *II*, p. 142

"must go one's . . ." *II*, p. 145

"kind of mystic . . ." *II*, p. 164

"TELL THIS . . ." *II*, p. 197

"They simply . . . ," "How can one . . ." *II*, p. 299

"I can *meet* . . ." *II*, p. 299 (corrected slightly for punctuation)

"What a relief . . . ," "the qualities . . . ," "cold bloodedly . . ." *II*, p. 137

"with a certain . . . ," "the *matter* . . . ," "show her . . ." *II*, p. 317

"a curious . . ." *II*, p. 318

"prayed on . . ." *II*, p. 336

"*roars* . . ." *II*, p. 337

"over the heads . . ." *II*, p. 338

"ill-natured . . ." *II*, p. 337

"awfully vulgar . . ." *II*, p. 339

"horror for . . ." *II*, p. 346

·10·

"a small amount . . ." *I*, p. 292

"A strange coldness . . ." *II*, p. 77

"You will live . . ." *I*, p. 135

"All intellectual . . . ," "Apparently . . . ," "Speaking of . . ." *II*, p. 175

"Kate afterwards . . ." *Wings*, pp. 40–41

"reversed every . . ." *III*, p. 220 (slight correction for punctuation)

"I went fizzling . . ." *III*, p. 220

"too much . . ." *Writings 1878–1899*, p. 829

"Americans who . . ." Ibid., p. 830

"the one . . . ," "into vivid . . ." *III*, p. 237

"What you say . . ." *III*, p. 239

"I thought . . ." *III*, p. 242

"It was a scant . . . ," "nothing of . . ." "The Manners of American Women," Henry James, *Harper's Bazaar* (April 1907), p. 355

"in the manners . . ." Ibid., p. 358

·11·

"a mere subject . . ." *I*, p. 153

"she has . . ." *I*, p. 154

"She seems . . ." *I*, p. 153

"*Cut out . . .*" *I*, p. 106

"young wom[e]n . . ." *Writings 1878–1899*, p. 948

"Women, we are . . ." "George Sand," Henry James, *Galaxy* (July 1877), p. 47

"*Exquisite* in . . ." *II*, p. 370

"women have . . ." *Terminations*, Henry James (New York: Harper & Brothers, 1995), p. 212

"Your young . . ." *I*, p. 47

"deepened the . . ." *The Bostonians*, Henry James (Kansas: Digireads.com, 2007), p. 123

"The young man . . ." *I*, p. 328

"Her insanity . . ." *I*, pp. 380–81

"I hope . . ." *I*, p. 381

"Nothing in . . ." "The Manners of American Women," Henry James, *Harper's Bazaar* (April 1907), p. 355

"no bottled-lightning . . ." *Writings 1878–1899*, p. 831
"Pauline is . . ." *III*, p. 65
"racing with . . ." *III*, p. 64
"much the . . ." *II*, p. 355
"No one . . ." *III*, p. 16
"Her father's life . . ." *Wings*, p. 3
"Our relatives . . ." *II*, pp. 359–360
"diff^t in . . ." *III*, p. 340
"For some . . . ," "It's impossible . . ." *III*, p. 341

·12·

"Masterly . . ." *II*, p. 89
"infinite talk . . . ," "acclaimed and . . . ," "twenty . . ." *The Art of the Novel: Critical Prefaces by Henry James*, Henry James (Chicago: University of Chicago Press, 2011), p. 184
"That's all . . ." *I*, p. 79
"I take up . . ." *I*, p. 175
"Do in writing . . ." *I*, p. 71
"Behold all . . ." *I*, p. 289
"Doing these . . ." *III*, p. 427
"of a large . . ." "George Sand," Henry James, *Galaxy* (July 1877), p. 52
"The spectacle . . ." *I*, p. 50

·13·

"Oh yes, . . ." *II*, p. 315
"gossiped to . . . ," "heroic in . . ." *II*, p. 311
"'coloured' . . ." *II*, p. 310
"I am troubled . . ." *II*, p. 315

"& then . . ." *II*, p. 311

"I don't see . . ." *II*, p. 317

"I have got . . ." *I*, p. 321

"a really . . ." *II*, p. 8

"I have done . . ." *II*, p. 7

"tenderly . . . ," "longer than . . ." *II*, p. 10

"The story is . . ." *II*, p. 9

"I trust . . ." *II*, p. 11

·14·

"It had great . . . ," "How worked . . ." *II*, p. 392

"The loveliest . . ." *Further Recollections of a Diplomatist*, Sir Horace Rumbold (London: Edward Arnold, 1903), p. 105

"You can't . . ." *The Selected Letters of Henry James*, ed. Leon Edel (New York: Farrar, Straus, and Giroux, 1999), p. 186

"great Psychist . . ." *II*, p. 392

"She was a . . ." *II*, p. 408

"That life is . . . ," "the lightness . . ." *Writings 1878–1899*, p. 484

"My task . . ." Ibid., p. 485

"Are you not . . . ," "She had . . ." *II*, p. 408

·15·

"I can't now . . ." *III*, p. 347 (corrected slightly)

"As an artist . . ." *III*, p. 393

"I have uttered . . ." *I*, p. 37

"I think it . . ." *I*, p. 176

"I hope you . . ." *I*, p. 308

"The multitude . . ." *I*, p. 170

"If *that's* . . ." *II*, p. 416

"It is superlatively . . ." *II*, p. 39
"But why won't . . ." *III*, p. 301
"I mean . . ." *III*, p. 305
"[it] goes agin . . ." *III*, p. 301
"Mine being . . ." *III*, p. 337
"I'm always sorry . . ." *III*, p. 305

·16·

"the powers . . ." *III*, p. 125
"I made an ass . . ." *III*, p. 125
"The chief . . ." *III*, p. 127
"The last boil . . ." *III*, p. 128
"There is *something* . . ." *III*, p. 310

·17·

"Gazing at your . . ." *II*, p. 123
"beautiful, innocent . . ." *III*, p. 51
"Perfect [thing] . . ." *II*, p. 41
"This is really . . ." *II*, p. 335
"very exquisite . . ." *III*, p. 114
"not 'ghosts' . . ." *The Turn of the Screw and Other Stories*, Henry
    James (Oxford: Oxford University Press, 1992), p. liii
"A queer pair . . ." *III*, p. 103
"You must . . ." *III*, p. 104

·18·

"The official . . ." *III*, p. 164
"the picturesque . . ." *Transatlantic Sketches*, Henry James (Bos-
    ton: James R. Osgood, 1875), p. 165

"This beautiful . . ." Ibid., pp. 165–166
"It comes from . . ." *I*, p. 321
"very old . . ." *Wings of the Dove*, p. v
"but half . . ." Ibid., p. xvi
"positively close . . ." Ibid., p. xix
"deeper draught . . ." Ibid., p. xv
"very much that . . ." Ibid., p. x
"a tide . . ." Ibid., p. 74
"plashes . . ." Ibid., p. 119
"against a firm . . ." Ibid., p. 289
"likened to the . . ." Ibid., p. 283
"All of which . . ." Ibid., pp. 382–383
"My stuff . . ." *III*, p. 222
"May you be . . ." *III*, p. 240

·19·

"[Roosevelt] gushes . . ." *Essays, Comments, and Reviews*, William James (Cambridge, Mass.: Harvard University Press, 1987), p. 163
"He swamps . . ." Ibid., p. 164
"*Terminato* . . ." *III*, p. 63
"wrapped up . . ." *I*, p. 286
"discredit[ed] in . . ." *Writings 1878–1899*, p. 745
"The old human . . ." *III*, p. 56
"Remarkable for . . ." *III*, p. 306
"Our ancestors . . ." *Writings 1902–1910*, p. 1283
"Rich men . . ." *I*, p. 178
"but one utopia . . ." *Writings 1902–1910*, p. 1284
"The military . . ." Ibid., p. 1291

"like a rat . . ." *III*, p. 311

"I would n't . . ." *III*, p. 313

"I am . . . as limp . . ." *III*, p. 313

"her taste . . ." *The Question*, p. 39

"to accept . . ." Ibid., pp. 24–25

"Keep up your . . ." Ibid., pp. 51–52

·20·

"The contents . . ." "The Letters of Honoré de Balzac," Henry
    James, *Galaxy* (February 1877), p. 183

"to see . . ." *Writings 1878–1899*, p. 491

"For three . . ." *I*, p. 366

"I come back . . ." *II*, p. 61

"Verily, it . . ." *I*, p. 116

"What a poor . . ." *I*, p. 189

"It's a horrible . . ." *I*, p. 142

"I write in . . ." *I*, p. 165

FIGURE CAPTIONS AND CREDITS

IMAGES OF LETTERS in both the front and the back of the book are used by permission of Houghton Library, Harvard University. Letter from W^m to H'ry, 8 September 1907, from William James papers, b MS Am 1092.9 (2938). Letter from H'ry to W^m, 17 October 1907, from Henry James papers, b MS Am 1094 (2203).

PAGE 3. From *The Correspondence of William James: William and Henry,* vol. 1 (Charlottesville: University Press of Virginia, 1992–1994), 4. Reprinted with the permission of Bay James.

PAGE 7. From *The Correspondence of William James: William and Henry,* vol. 2 (Charlottesville: University Press of Virginia, 1992–1994), 45. Reprinted with the permission of Bay James.

PAGE 16. Courtesy of the Houghton Library. Reprinted with the permission of Bay James.

PAGE 38. *Henry James*, John La Farge, 1862. Courtesy of the Century Association.

PAGE 45. *Presentation of the Virgin in the Temple,* Titian. Photo from Scala/Art Resource, New York. Used by permission.

PAGE 53. *The Palace of Sleep,* Gustavé Dore, 1870. Photo credit: Vintage-Views.com. Used by permission.

PAGE 55. *Paradise Valley, 1866–68,* John La Farge. Photo credit: Terra Foundation for American Art/Art Resource, New York. Used by permission.

PAGE 89. *Mrs. Mahlon Sands,* John Singer Sargent, 1894. From *John Singer Sargent: Portraits of the 1890s,* vol. 2 in Complete Paintings series (New Haven: Yale University Press, 2002). Used by permission.

INDEX

MUSE BOOKS

THE IOWA SERIES IN CREATIVITY AND WRITING

W^m & H'ry: Literature, Love, and the Letters
between William and Henry James
by J. C. Hallman

My Business Is to Create: Blake's Infinite Writing
by Eric G. Wilson